ONE FAMILY   ONE BODY   ONE HOUSE

THE HOUSE OF GOD
FASHIONED TO PLACE VALUE UPON HUMANITY

WITHOUT FAMILY,

MAN, ALONE IN THE WORLD TREMBLES WITH THE COLD

[ANDRE MACIROIS]

HUNGERING FOR REALITY...

BORN TO WORSHIP

THE RESCUE PLAN

LIGHT IN THE DARKNESS

JUSTICE PREVAILING

Light Justice

'I AM COME THAT YOU MIGHT HAVE LIFE,
AND LIFE MORE ABUNDANT.'

[JESUS CHRIST - JOHN 10:10]

MAKING MELODY
IN YOUR H E A R T

- 21ST CENTURY STYLE

FAMILY LOVE IS LIKE THE WIND:
INSTINCTIVE, RAW, FRAGILE, BEAUTIFUL,
AT TIMES ANGRY, BUT ALWAYS UNSTOPPABLE.
IT IS OUR COLLECTIVE BREATH. IT IS THE WORLD'S
GREATEST FORCE.

[JAMES MCBRIDE]

LIFE DELIGHTS IN
LIFE

"ONE THING
HAVE I DESIRED OF THE LORD,
THAT WILL I SEEK:
THAT I MAY DWELL IN THE HOUSE OF THE LORD
ALL THE DAYS OF MY LIFE,
TO BEHOLD THE BEAUTY OF THE LORD,
AND TO INQUIRE IN HIS TEMPLE.
FOR IN THE TIME OF TROUBLE
HE SHALL HIDE ME IN HIS PAVILION;
IN THE SECRET PLACE OF HIS TABERNACLE
HE SHALL HIDE ME;
HE SHALL SET ME HIGH UPON A ROCK.
AND NOW MY HEAD SHALL BE LIFTED UP
ABOVE MY ENEMIES ALL AROUND ME;
THEREFORE I WILL OFFER SACRIFICES OF JOY
IN HIS TABERNACLE;
I WILL SING, YES, I WILL SING PRAISES TO THE LORD."

[PSALM 27:4-6]

heaven is in this house

BOBBIE HOUSTON

PUBLISHED BY MAXIMISED LEADERSHIP INC.

HEAVEN IS IN THIS HOUSE
First published October 2001
Second impression February 2002

National Library of Australia:
Cataloguing-in-Publication data:

      Houston, Bobbie, 1957- .
      Heaven is in this house.

      ISBN 0 9577336 4 X.

      1. Heaven - Christianity. 2. Family - Religious aspects - Christianity. 3.
      Family - Psychological aspects. I. Title.

      236.24

Scripture quotations used in this book are from the following sources and used
with permission:
New King James Version (NKJV). Copyright © 1982, 1992 by Thomas
Nelson, Inc. Used by permission. All rights reserved.
The Amplified Bible (AMP). Old Testament Copyright © 1965,1987 by the
Zondervan Corporation. New Testament Copyright © 1958, 1987 by the
Lockman Foundation. Used by permission.
The Message (MSG). Copyright © 1993. Used with permission of NavPress
Publishing Group.
The Living Bible (TLB). Copyright © 1971 by Tyndale House Publishers.

Bold emphasis or capitalisation in certain scriptures is the author's own.

Dictionary definitions taken from the Oxford Concise Australian Dictionary

Cover design by Richard Pritchard, Sydney Media Collective

Inside photographs: Various Hillsong Church people as captured by Bobbie
Houston, Femia Shirtliff, and others

Printed by J S McMillan Printing, Lidcombe NSW Australia

Published by Maximised Leadership Incorporated,
PO Box 1195, Castle Hill, NSW 1765 Australia

MY HEART'S DESIRE

To love the Lord my God with all my heart, all
my soul, all my strength.

That the people in my world will also love this
Saviour with all their heart, soul,
and strength.

And that when the rewards are being handed
out in Heaven, not one person will be missing.

ALWAYS GRATEFUL

I will be eternally grateful to my husband, children and God family for making my world so colourful and full. (Brian, Joel, Ben, Laura, Hillsong Church and friends – this is actually a brag-book about you.)

Special gratitude to those loyal friends who faithfully work alongside and enable us to continually push out the boundaries. You are too many to number but Heaven is definitely taking notes. I will love you forever.

This book is dedicated to the beautiful memory of Elizabeth (Lilly) Greatbach, who courageously introduced me to Jesus and His magnificent Kingdom.

CONTENTS

IRRESISTIBLE!

EARTH IS CRAMMED WITH
HEAVEN
[ELIZABETH BARRETT BROWNING]

AND LOVE ALWAYS PREVAILS

IRRESISTIBLE!

Once upon a time, a magnificent son left home. He travelled to a distant place to fulfil his father's dream. He established new friends, a new family, and a new life. One day, his friends asked him about his former home. Their hearts yearned to understand. So this magnificent son taught them a prayer that would bring what he knew into their world. His prayer sounded like this … "Awesome Father in Heaven, You are so wonderful, so hallowed, so beloved. Cause Your Kingdom and Your amazing Will to come from Heaven to this place, so that my friends might also experience what we know."

This magnificent son is of course, our Lord and Saviour Jesus Christ, and the prayer is the Lord's Prayer found in Matthew chapter six. If you are a believer reading this book, then like myself, you are born anew and Heaven bound, but until that day comes, you and I have a responsibility to bring Heaven to earth. We have a responsibility to establish 'His Will' and 'His Kingdom' down here – to build 'His House' in such a way that mankind is given a little *pre-glimpse* of Heaven.

A person unfamiliar with the goodness of God might ask, "So what does God look like?" Good question, considering many of us may have *felt* His touch, but have not literally *seen* Him face to face. My humble answer is, "Well … take everything on the planet that is wonderful, good, beautiful, tender, precious, delightful, colourful, fresh, exuberant and inspirational…" and we may have a minuscule glimpse of this amazing God.

Do you ever stop and wonder about Heaven? Do you ever ponder, "I wonder what it actually sounds like? I wonder what it smells like? What does it really look like? What do they do up there all day, or for all of eternity? Do they ever get face-ache from smiling? How about the music? Is it soft or loud? How about the food? What does one wear in Heaven ... and hey, do those mansions really exist?"

To be honest, I do not spend all of my time wondering about Heaven, but I am seriously interested because I believe the House of God down here on planet earth (the Church) should reflect the atmosphere, energy, life and goodness of the House of God in Heaven.

Is that too large a statement to digest? Think about it for a moment. Jesus prayed, "Thy Will be done, Thy Kingdom come on earth as it is in Heaven" (Matthew 6: 9). **I believe the Church on the earth today should reflect Heaven.** I realise we are comparing a natural and a spiritual dimension, yet *our local churches* should echo Heaven. They should echo the joy and warmth of Heaven. They should echo the life, sound, peace and presence of a place **where God Himself dwells**, because God inhabits the praises of His people (Psalm 22:3).

Heaven should not be a remote, distant, obscure or even mystical concept. When God's people love and worship Him, the Word declares that He rides the heavens and comes and dwells among us. That sounds like Heaven to me! When God arrives, everything about Him arrives too – His goodness, grace, blessing, abundance, joy, excellence, magnificence, power and fullness.

I personally find that thought **irresistible.** I think the **House of God should be irresistible** – like a giant magnet, drawing people into its warmth and light. In fact, I am totally in love with this idea and this book is an attempt to provide a glimpse of where I feel the Church is heading.

You see, I love this House (God's Church). I fell in love with it the moment I entered through its doors. Who wouldn't? I met my Saviour, my world was turned around and the curtains were drawn back to reveal the adventure I am living today. My life is given to this Cause and I continually ask the Father to allow me to see and understand His heartbeat regarding both His people and His House.

I earnestly desire to see it from Heaven's perspective, so that we (His people) can be diligent in building His Church **as He would have us build it.** I'm also anxious to know what His Church will look like as this amazing 21st Century unfolds.

Irresistible! ... Great word isn't it?

Allow me to ask you some questions, keeping in mind that the moment of salvation is merely *the starting point* of a great journey with God. Is your Christianity irresistible? Is your testimony and walk with God irresistible to those around you? Are they drawn to you like a magnet? Do they smile when they see you coming? Is the place where you worship irresistible? Does it stand out in your community? Do the unredeemed community around you perhaps scratch their head as they observe your church in action? They may not understand, and they may not have yet entered through your doors, but are they at least wondering: What goes on in there? Why are marriages restored? Why are people healed or cured of addictions? Why are they so happy?

I do not believe the unsaved world should drive past our churches and not even notice them. There should be something that catches their attention, turns their head and makes them wonder, "What on earth is going on in there? Why is this place overflowing with people? What is it with all these young people? Why are there so many cars? What is that warmth, love and sound of laughter? Is something happening that I don't know about?"

The answer is YES! Heaven has come to earth!

A dear friend from the United States was visiting our church during one of our annual conferences. At the end of two weeks of extensive meetings and celebrations, she staggered upstairs and affectionately announced, "Blessed are those who endure to the end!" The conference had been *so good* that nobody wanted to let the singing, dancing and rejoicing end. Then she said something that helped inspire the title of this book, "I didn't know Heaven was in Australia!"

This comment was actually more profound than our friend Nancy Alcorn had realised. Heaven had indeed come to Australia. For two weeks, God's presence, goodness, grace and joy had saturated the conference and all those who attended. Thousands of delegates had pulled God into their world and His presence had been irresistible – so irresistible that nobody wanted to go home.

I believe this is how the House of God should always be. So **irresistible** and **functional** that people cannot wait to get there and then once there, never want to leave.

This book is an attempt to **stir your heart**. It is not an exhaustive endeavour designed to unravel the theological mysteries of the Kingdom, the Tabernacle, the

Sanctuary or the Holy of Holies. Rather it is an attempt to paint a simple, yet powerful picture of what Heaven on earth might look like in your community, city and nation. I am using the simple analogy of Family, Body and House and will relate it from our own experience here in Sydney.

This passion for the House of God burns in my heart because I once heard a friend say, "Life is short, eternity is long, Heaven is real, hell is hot and our message is Jesus." Somehow that puts it all in perspective, doesn't it? So lean forward, relax and may His grace allow you and me to be moved beyond our world and into another.

CHAPTER ONE

THE HILLSONG STORY [SO FAR]

YOU ARE MY WORLD

[TOGETHER IN THE SYDNEY ENTERTAINMENT CENTRE, MARCH 2001]

THE HILLSONG STORY [SO FAR]

STORY — A NARRATIVE, TALE, ACCOUNT
OF A JOURNEY TRAVELLED.

For some wonderful reason God has chosen to smile upon my husband, myself and the awesome company of people who constitute the Hillsong Church. Many years of being knit together have produced 'influence' that is not only bearing fruit at a local and national level, but also at a global level. Our being knit together into **one house, one body** and **one family** has produced a message that God has chosen to take beyond our four walls.

As young newlweds leaving New Zealand to join the new church plant in Sydney, Brian and I were full of dreams, yet I don't know that any of those involved in the early pioneer days could have envisioned the extent of the influence. In 1977 the original vision statement was *'Our city and beyond.'* I remember a dear friend once said, "If you love a suburb, God will give you the city; if you love the city, He'll give you the nation; and if you love the nation, He will give you the nations." We immediately fell madly in love with the city of Sydney and as we have laboured to give our best to her, God has added the 'beyond' to our world.

Life is truly a 'story, a narrative and tale of a journey travelled.' When you are young and a little green around the gills, you generally don't find people lining up to glean from your experience. However if you stay true to your heart, true to the vision and above all, true to the Word of God, the picture changes dramatically. We may not have consciously sought this influence in the beginning, but as it has emerged and grown in stature and respect, we have certainly and unapologetically become stewards over the opportunity given to us.

The Hillsong story has never been written before and in all honesty, this book is not intended for that purpose. I am going to leave that honour to my husband to write one day. My heart for this book is to give **church leaders and believers** alike, a glimpse of what 'their House' could (or perhaps needs to) look like, and of course in the process of painting this picture, I will naturally glean from our experience.

I love our church. It is by no means perfect. It has by no means 'arrived' but for me, it is a living, breathing expression of my God. It is full of His amazing kids and because the Church is His first love, it naturally becomes my first love too. Our church (like yours) is *God's first love*. The Church is the object of His affection, attention, gaze and grace. I sense God's face is towards the Hillsong Church, because the heartbeat and soul of our church is ever towards His face. We have tasted of His favour, we are blessed and we are growing in the revelation of all this wonder.

So ... are we more blessed than others? Are we among His favourites? Did we stumble across some magic formula? No! We are simply a bunch of kids who fell in love with God and devoted ourselves to having a go. We chose never to lose our child-likeness, and somewhere in that simple equation, the Hillsong Church has emerged. She is, by God's grace, endeavouring to reach her local community, and along the way became a benchmark that others are choosing to pattern themselves after.

Are we unique on the earth? No! God is moving all over the planet, doing wonderful things in many contexts and cultures. Yet God throughout history has been known to shine His light on certain pockets of His Church at different times. He has been known to pull out a highlighter and mark some in such a way that others might notice what has Heaven's attention.

In a nutshell, what is it that draws people from all over the world to 'our House'? Each week we find ourselves host to visitors from all corners of the earth. What is so special about a local Sydney church on a little street corner in a nation that is affectionately known as the Land Down Under? Is it the worship? Is it the strength of the leadership? Is it the dynamic of the emerging youth generation? Is it the spirit of servanthood? What causes the magnetic pull? What separates her and what earns her this reputation?

I believe the magnet is her **heart and soul**. The heart or the very core of this church is *healthy* and very much *in love with her Saviour*. Yes, the music is special – it has emerged as a fresh new sound from Heaven above and is marked with a unique anointing. Yes, the leaders are strong – a team of excellent men and women, not fully perfected yet, but uncomplicated in style and in application. Yes, there is the sound of an emerging youth generation. An army of young people – passionate, zealous, adventurous, not bound by religious traditions, wired differently from any generation before them, who are determined to take today's youth culture and expose it to an unrestrained Jesus Revolution. Yet central to all of this, is a **healthy heart**. The SPIRIT OF THE HOUSE is what the Father is drawing attention to. The Word says, "Beloved, I pray that you might prosper and be in health, *even as your soul prospers*" (John 3:2).

The **spirit and soul** of the Hillsong Church is the **gold** at the end of the rainbow. Many people are looking for a formula or method for growth, yet let me say that *singing our songs* as a formula won't do it. Singing great songs will definitely help, but it has to go deeper than simply mimicking someone else's style. Our songs are actually an expression of our health in God. *Copying our programs and events* also won't do it. Efforts in this area are merely our tools to let our sphere of influence know that there is a God in Heaven who loves them. Every individual church needs to look intelligently at the needs of her community and act accordingly. Our *pattern of teaching* also won't do it, because words without revelation, a spirit of love and genuine concern for people are merely words – they carry no fresh breath of the Holy Spirit that in turn yields life. Our challenge as leaders is to always bring fresh life to the people in our sphere of influence.

I believe that across the earth in various places and amongst various people, God is highlighting 'keys' that can **turn His House and His Church into a living, breathing expression of Heaven on earth.** He yearns for humanity to realise and unearth the dynamic that is 'His House.' His Church is not a building. It is not a program or an event, nor a gospel television program for that matter. It is not even Sunday or weekend services that gather believers. His House is the *tangible framework that embraces and cherishes His people which then causes them to flourish in life.* Of course we need buildings and programs to function, and television is a crucial 21st Century medium for the extension of His truth, but I am talking about something deeper.

One day during worship I asked the Lord to show me His heartbeat concerning

His Church. I sensed the Spirit of God respond to my request with this precise answer. "Bobbie, when I look at my beautiful people, I call them three things. I call them **a Family**, **a Body** and **a House**." Then I felt the Spirit say, "When I call them a Family, it is about *unconditional love and acceptance*. When I call them a Body, it is about *effective function* and when I call them a House, it is about *reaching the world*." Then I felt the Holy Spirit say, "Teach it."

So here I am. Not pretending to be anything that I am not, but simply penning the conviction of my heart. The following pages will simply paint the picture as I see it. The exciting truth is that revelation has the capacity to refine and expand in our understanding. God's Word says, "The path of the just shines brighter and brighter unto the perfect day" (Proverb 4:18).

Well – that perfect day when we shall all see Him face to face is drawing closer, and without doubt, the 'mysteries of the Kingdom' are becoming clearer and clearer. This book will be wonderfully dated before it is even printed, because the path that we are all walking is a 'work in progress.' With each new day, the **revelation** refines, the **mandate** becomes clearer and the **adventure** becomes more attainable. I realise that for many, what I am hinting at may seem like an unrealistic ideal because their environment is far removed from this analogy. For that reason I understand and declare that **this responsibility rests on both people and leaders alike to chase and secure.** So don't despair, be faithful and be patient, and live in hope that a new day is dawning.

Between you and me, I can't wait for the future to unfold. So stay with me as we put our God-given imagination to work.

OUR FATHER IN HEAVEN,
HALLOWED BE YOUR NAME.

YOUR KINGDOM COME.

YOUR WILL BE DONE
ON EARTH AS IT IS IN HEAVEN.

GIVE US THIS DAY OUR DAILY BREAD.

AND FORGIVE US OUR DEBTS,

AS WE FORGIVE OUR DEBTORS.

AND DO NOT LEAD US INTO TEMPTATION,
BUT DELIVER US FROM THE EVIL ONE.

FOR YOURS IS THE KINGDOM AND THE
POWER AND THE GLORY FOREVER.

AMEN.

[MATTHEW 6:9-13]

CHAPTER TWO

SONS AND DAUGHTERS ON
A JOURNEY HOME

HOMEWARD
BOUND!

SONS AND DAUGHTERS ON
A JOURNEY HOME

"I go to prepare a place for you." This beautiful, heartfelt statement is among the final, earthly words of Jesus. He had come from Heaven to earth, He had lived among us for a moment and He was about to execute the ultimate RESCUE PLAN. The season ahead would be traumatic and exhausting for those close to Him, so He deposited peace into their souls with words that hopefully would come to their remembrance.

At the risk of being elementary to some, I am going to paint a picture that hopefully will take the mystery out of life. I can still remember what it felt like to live with a question mark over life. I can still articulate the questions: "Why am I here?", "Surely there is more to life than living sixty, seventy, eighty years and then death?" and "Why do I have this sense of dissatisfaction?"

When I was fourteen years of age, my father died and I could not come to grips with the thought that he no longer existed. He had to exist. How could such a kind, generous and wonderful human being suddenly be reduced to crematorium ash? To my young mind, his spirit had to exist somewhere. I would often draw back the night curtains of my bedroom, gaze at the stars and hope that somewhere out there, my precious father still remained.

Ecclesiastes 3:11 declares that eternity is etched within our hearts:

> "He has made everything beautiful in its time. *He also has planted eternity in men's hearts and minds* [a divinely implanted sense of a purpose working through the ages which nothing under the sun but God alone can satisfy]"

I hadn't read or been taught these verses at fourteen years of age, yet my heart seemed well aware of them. Eternity is definitely written within us. It is our eternal (and internal) 'homing device' – the force that, if permitted, will draw us back into the arms of a loving heavenly Father. So allow me to paint a simple picture of 'the Plan' – the plan that embraces eternity, time, the Creator and YOU. The plan that watches your every move and lives in hope of your perfect response. The plan that has woven itself across the centuries and now involves you, me and our local community.

THE PLAN

In the beginning God created us. Our origin began when God the Father, God the Son and God the Holy Spirit said, "Let us make man in OUR image" (Genesis 1:26). He created a *man-person* from the dust of the earth and named him Adam. (Our finite minds can only imagine, but I am rather hoping that God has kept 'home movies' of all this and after the big marriage supper of the Lamb in Heaven, we will all sit down and watch in wonder at how it all really happened.)

As perfect as Adam must have been, the scene was not quite perfect enough. A 'helper' suitable (or perfect) for Adam could not be found, so God had another amazing idea. He caused His newly created SON to fall asleep and then with a stroke of genius, fashioned a partner and playmate out of Adam's flesh. This woman, this DAUGHTER, this stunning twice-refined creation would complete the plan and her name would be Eve. Together they would rule and reign and be highly successful. Together they would walk in close communion with their Creator. Together they had the capacity to create and pro-create. Together they could function in the true image of God.

God's heart lent towards them and He *entrusted and dignified* them with the POWER OF CHOICE.

THE PLAN INTERRUPTED

Choice characterises humanity. You and I have a will – the power to choose between LIFE and DEATH (Deuteronomy 30:19). We all face a moment of choice, which determines our eternal future, and Adam and Eve were no different. Somewhere in 'their journey' they faced the moment that defined not only their future, but OURS as well, because we were tucked away in their loins.

God had placed them in a perfect environment and had given them ONE instruction. Tragically 'the enemy' came and successfully tricked them into violating that one instruction. The enemy is Satan. Often referred to as the devil, he was once a powerful and influential angel in Heaven, known by the name of Lucifer. Choice was also within his power. He chose to rebel, he chose to set himself up against the Creator of the universe and he found himself cast to earth and hell (Isaiah 14). Such was Lucifer's influence that the Bible says he seduced a third of the angels to go with him. Hell was not created for God's precious sons and daughters – it was created for Satan and his cohorts. His time on earth is numbered and his mission is to make tangible his hatred. He knows how magnificent Heaven is, he knows what 'home' looks like and his obsession is to blind, deceive and prevent humanity from experiencing what he knew and **lost**. Jesus said that "the thief does not come except to steal, and to kill, and to destroy" (John 10:10).

For that reason, he sought to and succeeded in interrupting 'the Plan.' He deceived the man and the woman and plunged us all into a scenario that required a desperately needed redemptive plan. In the 'process of time' Jesus Christ entered the picture and Heaven orchestrated the ultimate RESCUE PLAN of the ages. The perfect Son of God laid down His life for the likes of you and me.

THE PLAN RESTORED

So two thousand years ago our King came, established Salvation and returned to Heaven. He released the Holy Spirit into our midst and handed the keys of the Kingdom to us. *Here enters the Church of the Living God. Here enters the Church of Jesus Christ – the Family of God, the Body of God and the House of God* (Refer to John 3:16; Acts 2 and Matthew 16:18).

The master plan of walking lost humanity *home to Heaven* has been placed within the hands of those who have made Jesus Christ their Lord, and who have responded to a Saviour who declared, "I am the Way, the Truth and the Life. No man comes to the Father except through Me" (John 14:6).

The Church of Jesus Christ today, has the awesome privilege (and challenge) of reaching a planet that is thronging with humanity. I am told that there are more people *alive today* (drawing breath right now) than have ever lived and died up until now. That means that we have **the possibility and responsibility of swinging eternity in favour of heaven.** We are living in THE most exciting times ever. Never before has the Church been more equipped, more resourced and more empowered to make a difference. Without doubt society is broken down in many places and the planet is groaning under the weight of severe injustice, which results so often because of the fight between Light and Darkness, but the entire tenor of the Word of God and Salvation's plan is to CORRECT THAT WHICH IS WRONG.

Unbelievers are often heard to say, "Well, if He's such a God of love, how come there is so much pain the world?" The answer: because the Church (over the centuries) in many ways lost sight of her commission. She became broken down and weak. She forgot that she was supposed to be strong and authoritative. She forgot she was supposed to offer Truth to common people in such a way that it actually brought liberty, freedom and success to their everyday lives. She forgot her doors were always supposed to be open. She forgot she was supposed to be **the living expression of God's heavenly family – a reflection of Heaven to a lost and dying world.** She also forgot that she was designed to be THE most magnetic force in society – attractive, warm, inviting, relevant – so much so that the sons and daughters of planet earth cannot help but stop and be drawn within her walls. As our friend Nancy Alcorn from Mercy Ministries so poignantly puts it, "God did not anoint government to heal the broken-hearted, **He anointed the Church!"**

OUR PART

So how does all this work? How can we simplify the equation so that EVERY BELIEVER understands how essential they are to the House of God and the big picture of rescuing a rapidly destructing planet? 1 Timothy 3:15 gives expression to God's heart and the framework of this plan. Amid a New Testament full of instruction and principles on how to live brilliantly, we find a verse that says:

> "I write these things unto you, *so that you may know how to conduct yourselves* in the HOUSE OF GOD, which is the CHURCH OF THE LIVING GOD, the very PILLAR AND GROUND OF TRUTH."

This verse declares that the Church is the **pillar and foundation of Truth on the earth**. In other words, the Church as a pillar and foundation is capable of holding up and stabilising life in a struggling and turbulent world. However, this will not happen to the degree that God yearns for *if we as believers do not learn how to powerfully connect and function as the Body of Christ.*

According to the passage just quoted, YOU AND I constitute 'the Church.' The Church is definitely not a building, but when we (flesh and blood) gather to the building, the building suddenly becomes 'the House of God.' When we leave and the lights go out, it is merely a building again, but while we are there it BECOMES

THE HOUSE OF GOD. This House has the capacity to be magnificent, wonderful and awesome. It has the capacity to carry an anointing from above that can fulfill all of His purposes in all of our lives and it has the capacity to make a difference in the world.

This may sound fundamental to many of you, but it will also be revelation to many. So many churches and Christians fall short of their potential because they allow themselves to have a *casual relationship* with their church not realising that they are actually FAMILY, BODY AND HOUSE designed to do life together.

God's desire is to write abundant health across every aspect of life. We are all **sons and daughters on a journey home** and **our successful arrival**, with everyone and everything in place, hinges on each and every individual House or church across the earth effectively rising to their full stature and influence. It hinges on us creating an awesome environment in church life that can lift the ceiling off people and cause them to flourish. As the Word says, "those who are planted in the House of God shall flourish" (Psalm 92:13).

The first part of this book takes the analogy of a 'healthy natural family' and paints it into God's spiritual family. It is a simple yet powerful analogy because FAMILY is actually the very essence of who God is. The Word describes Him as Heavenly Father, nurturing Mother, Bridegroom, Husband and Brother. And ... because He is family, the Church, above and before anything else, should also be family.

'Let your heart not be
troubled; you believe in
God, believe also in Me.

In my Father's house are
many mansions; if it were
not so, I would have told
you. I go to prepare a
place for you.

And if I go and prepare a
place for you, I will come
again and receive you to
myself; that where I am,
there you may be also.'

[JOHN 14:1-3]

PART ONE

'I CALL YOU FAMILY!'

FAMILY — A BROTHERHOOD OF
PEOPLE AND NATIONS, A CELEBRATION OF LIFE!

HEALTHY FAMILIES PRODUCE MAGNIFICENT, FUNCTIONAL HUMAN BEINGS

MAGNIFICENT – SPLENDID, IMPOSING, IMPRESSIVE, EXCELLENT

HEALTHY FAMILIES PRODUCE MAGNIFICENT, FUNCTIONAL HUMAN BEINGS

TO PRODUCE — TO BRING INTO EXISTENCE

Betty Johnston is a wonderful woman on our pastoral team. One day she was heard to say, "There is no reason anyone should leave this church – why would anyone leave a functional family?" A mind-blowing concept for some to get their heads around, but full of truth nonetheless. Whoever in their right mind would *resist* or *walk away* from a **magnificent, functional family full of unconditional love and acceptance?**

However, this is sadly where many churches have fallen short and still do. As already stated, many people, for whatever reason, allow themselves to have a *casual relationship* with their church, not realising we are actually **family designed to 'do life' together**. For some, the moment challenge presents itself, they bail out and then wonder why life is not unfolding as it should. The reality is they have disconnected themselves from the company of people with whom God the Father intended them to 'do life.'

Imagine if my eldest son took this attitude. Suppose Joel never grasped the revelation that his parents, siblings and extended natural and God-family were connected to his *pre-designed destiny path*. Imagine if at the first bend in the road, he hit a 'dysfunctional moment' and decided, "That's it! I'm leaving. I'll just go and join another family" or "I'll just do it on my own." This may seem a silly scenario, but nevertheless it is very real for many, and is far too common across the landscape of the Church. We have been in ministry for over 25 years and have witnessed too many people shipwreck themselves and their families because of this crazy attitude. Our responsibility is to change the world and create an environment where dysfunction is quickly dealt with and replaced with a way of living that is nothing less than magnificent.

MAGNIFICENT

Language is fascinating. It is the written and spoken medium by which we communicate and give expression to our hearts. Words are also very powerful and creative. For example, God spoke and everything we see and know came into existence! (Now there's a thought that deserves more than a sentence.) The word 'magnificent' is sweet to my ears and constantly on my lips. It is actually one of the many words used to define the glory of God, and within its meaning are the words *splendid, imposing, impressive* and *excellent*.

I actually believe that **healthy families produce magnificent (splendid, imposing, impressive and excellent) human beings.** Not necessarily *perfect* human beings because all our individual journeys are not complete until we each take our last breath, but without doubt, *splendid, imposing, impressive* and *excellent* human beings emerge from environments that are basically healthy. In observing life, one does not generally find such people emerging from broken, neglected, unharmonious or dysfunctional backgrounds. Now that doesn't mean they cannot. The human spirit has the capacity, and has been known to surface triumphant from the most hideous of situations, but more often than not, such negative environments sadly leave their mark.

Many of you reading this book could testify to being raised in such surroundings, yet today you stand strong and healed and anything but dysfunctional. So what happened? What changed the scenario? More than likely, **you changed families**. You found yourself confronted with *a choice*. You chose Christ and found yourself born again into a brand new, heavenly family … GOD'S FAMILY! You found yourself restored to a Heavenly Father who is magnificent and your life began to flourish.

FLOURISHING

'The [uncompromisingly] righteous shall flourish like a palm tree [be long-lived, stately, upright, useful and fruitful]; they shall grow like a cedar in Lebanon [majestic, stable, durable, and incorruptible]. Planted in the house of the Lord, they shall flourish in the courts of our God. [Growing in grace] they shall still bring forth fruit in old age; they shall be full of sap [of spiritual vitality] and [rich in the] verdure [of trust, love and contentment]. [They are living memorials] to show that the Lord is upright and faithful to His promises; He is my Rock, and there is no unrighteousness in Him' (Pslam 92:12-15 AMP)

So here's the deal: With all my heart, I believe that *healthy, functional, spiritual* CHURCH FAMILIES cannot help but produce *healthy, functional and spiritually* MAGNIFICENT PEOPLE who flourish in life. God never intended His Church to be reduced to *a mere centre* that people visit. Even as a natural family would fall short if they took this attitude, so too believers often *fall short of their God-given potential* because they never grasp this simple yet powerful revelation. God always intended His beloved Church to be the framework that would wrap people in an environment that would produce magnificent maturity on both the natural and spiritual level.

Generally speaking, **beautiful, functional adults** are simply **beautiful children who made a choice and allowed themselves to GROW UP.** *Unconditional agape love* (acceptance based on who people are) and *loving discipleship* (which trains tender hearts into maturity) produces magnificent human beings ... and magnificent human beings are what this planet so desperately groans for.

A couple of years ago, our youth held their annual Summer Camp. These camps are awesome moments where hundreds of teenagers get together, rage, surf and vent their youthful energy. They have a great time and above and beyond anything else, they love and embrace their Creator in such a way that Heaven invades their humble tent city on a rugged beach north of Sydney.

The Sunday after this particular camp, my husband Brian (being the spontaneous pastor he is) decided it would be fun to have 'Surf Sunday' at church. Hey, it was January in Australia – everyone was in holiday mode and to be honest we only do bizzare things like this once in a blue moon (not!). So the deal was to come to church in beach gear, Hawaiian shirt, boardies, Aussie thongs (jandals), or whatever made you happy (bikinis excluded). The night would be fun and the youth could testify about Summer Camp.

As the service unfolded, one young man in particular stood up and captured everyone's attention with his testimony and sheer confidence in front of the large

SUMMER CAMP

... AND STANDING ON YOUR HEAD
FOR NO REASON!

congregation. A visiting pastor (obviously not in surf gear) afterwards exclaimed, "…That young man who spoke, he's incredible, what a gift, what confidence, amazing, you need to *mark* that young man, he's got potential written all over him". My response was "Absolutely!" But then I found myself also saying, "But do you want to know something – this church is FULL of young people just like him. They are ALL amazing!"

Now what was I really saying? Was absolutely every single young person brilliant? Of course not! As gorgeous as every single one of them is, they are definitely not all there yet! Was I trying to draw attention to our brilliance as pastors? I don't think so! Without God's grace we'd all be in a pickle! No! I was drawing attention to a **church family,** that to the best of her ability so far, is pedantic about producing an atmosphere of unconditional love and acceptance. An atmosphere which embraces young people in a totally unreligious yet uncompromising way and is committed to seeing them emerge into normal, healthy young people who are *equipped to love life and love God with all their heart.*

MAGNETIC

Trust me, the world is looking for them. The week following, a national television network phoned our office enquiring as to whether we *just might* have any young people, who *just might* be choosing to abstain from premarital sex. They wanted to interview some young people on national television because there was, according to them, "a bit of interest out there about young people who in this day and age are choosing to live within certain moral boundaries."

Our world is looking for impressive, imposing, excellent human beings (young and old alike) who have the courage to stand and live by convictions that don't end in dysfunction and brokenness. I love it! Pockets of society may glamourise sin as much as they wish. They may sneer at what they *perceive* Christianity to be, but in the coming days, more than at any other time in history, it will be this emerging and strengthening Church who will gladly bandage and mend the broken lives that result from living outside the safe parameters of healthy natural and spiritual family.

Old fasioned Mother Nature (uninterfered with) places newborn individuals within the tender framework of natural family. **Salvation's plan** is to take those precious individual families and place them within the same tender framework of spiritual Christ-like family (ie: the House of God/the Church). And I am convinced that the original God-inspired qualities and principles that constitute *healthy life and therefore family* have the capacity to produce magnificence on every level. The outcome – splendid, imposing, impressive and excellent people who are discovering how to extract the marrow out of life.

When it comes to people, *excellence* and *perfection* are two very different things. Perfection is something which people can sadly strive for, without realising that the audience that really matters (Heaven) isn't asking for perfection. Excellence, on the other hand, is something that becomes almost second nature or consequential in environments that simply **believe in people**. God isn't looking for perfection (yet), but rather our wholehearted effort, which in turn allows Him *to perfect His work in us.*

> 'And I am convinced and sure of this very thing, that He Who began a good work in you will continue until the day of Jesus Christ [right up to the time of His return], developing [that good work] and perfecting and bringing it to full completion in you.' (Philippians 1:6 AMP)

I believe the **Family of God (within the framework of the House of God),** has the potential to draw these magnificent qualities out of men and women regardless of age. The key is to firstly harness God's enabling power on a personal level in our own lives, and then to offer our best to those alongside us.

Our dear friends Mark and Darlene Zschech recently welcomed a new little bundle into their world. As Brian and I stood with Darlene at the foot of her bed and watched little one-week-old Zoe Jewel awaken from sleep, Darlene described the reaction of her other daughters to their new sister. Chloe had been lost for words – she didn't know how to articulate what she was feeling. On the other hand, Amy knew exactly how to express it. To her listening and doting grandmother she had said, "Grandie, I'm going to do everything I can to give my new baby sister *a beautiful life!*" How lovely is that! And not only will little Zoe Jewel be lavished to *extravagant* lengths with love by her own natural family, but she'll be lavished upon by the spiritual family in which she is planted. So how can this child therefore not emerge magnificent on the planet!

I love this picture!

CHAPTER FOUR

HEALTHY FAMILIES PRODUCE SUPERNATURAL PEOPLE

PERFECTION –

LOVE GOD, LOVE PEOPLE, LOVE LIFE

HEALTHY FAMILIES PRODUCE SUPERNATURAL PEOPLE

GOD-IDEA — A CONCEPTION OR PLAN OF INTENTION AND PURPOSE

———————

L et me say it again – FAMILY is a SUPERNATURAL GOD IDEA. Family is not some bureaucratic administrative system that government invented to keep tabs on people. "Okay, your first name is ... , your surname ... , and oh yes, you live with these other people at *such and such* an address". No! Family has its origin in God. It is a God-conceived, God-breathed, God-inspired heavenly gift that if embraced, **carries an anointing from above that can yield the sweetest fruit.** Little babies just don't arrive out of thin air. They are birthed into the loving embrace of family and God's intention is that they flourish in life.

In Ephesians 3, the Word explains how we can experience life:

"For this reason I bow my knees to the Father of our Lord Jesus Christ, *from whom the whole family in Heaven and earth is named,* that He would grant you, according to the riches of His glory, to be strengthened with might through His Spirit in the inner man, that Christ may dwell in your hearts through faith; that you, *being rooted and grounded in love,* may be able to comprehend with all the saints what is the width and length and depth and height – to know the love of Christ which passes knowledge; that you may be filled with all the fullness of God."

(Ephesians 3:14-21)

SUPER ON OUR NATURAL

Naturally speaking, when a man and a woman fall in love and commit to marriage, God witnesses and acknowledges this union, extending to them a name that in essence belongs to Him – FAMILY! I'll use our history as an example. On the 19th February 1977 Mr Brian Houston and Miss Bobbie McDonald (don't laugh☺) suddenly became Mr & Mrs Brian Houston. From Heaven's perspective we became a unit, a family, and an extension now of the Houston family line.

Suddenly two became *one flesh* - one body, one family, one house. Suddenly our natural lives were **supernaturally knit together.** An unseen dynamic took place when the minister pronounced us man and wife. What would affect one would *supernaturally* now affect the other. What defined, built or blessed one partner would define, build or bless the other; and what had the potential to hurt, injure or come against one, could and would be felt by the other partner.

A Heaven-inspired and Heaven-witnessed **covenant** is entered into, which is why marriage breakdown is so painful. It is the tearing apart of a flesh covenant and regardless of how vehemently anti-God philosophy discredits its value, its breakdown is nevertheless heartbreak that the Father never intended us to experience. Any honest person who has experienced marital breakdown will agree and tell you how painful it is.

When the Bible says that God hates divorce, we are not suggesting that divorce cannot or won't happen (refer to Malachi 2:14-16). The Word recognises that the human heart has the capacity to fall short, and even be 'deceitfully evil' if it so chooses (see Jeremiah 17:9), but what God the Father hates is the *pain* it brings to the family involved. He also knows that when hearts are willing and teachable, any marriage breakdown can be healed and restored.

So when two individuals come together (as we did), and when they choose to reproduce in their marriage the *nature of God's divine family* (i.e. endeavour to live according to His principles) then I believe *an anointing from above will rest upon that natural family and the fruit will be supernatural.* In other words, the children that emerge from that household will not be average, run-of-the-mill kids. Oh, they'll be kids in every sense of the word, but they will have a supernatural *something* about them that will separate them from those who choose to live outside God's way.

Brian and I have three kids – two fabulous sons and a truly delightful daughter.

When Laura was little, she was shy, bashful and lacked confidence which is not really unusual for little children. But one day, out of the blue, she came home from school and announced, "Mummy, I've decided I'm just going to be confident… and I'm going to help other children be confident also". With that bold afternoon statement she changed – overnight! The shy, retiring little girl ceased to exist.

Where did that enabling come from? (It took me thirty years to overcome my shyness.) It came from a little girl who lives in an *environment* that whilst very down-to-earth and normal, is not natural, *but supernatural.* She is surrounded with Godly encouragement, and each week at church and in her youth group she hears the Word taught in a language she can understand. She has also grown up in an atmosphere of praise and worship, which basically means the presence of God has had *access* to her little heart. Put all that together and you have a moment when the anointing came and turned a little girl's natural confidence into something *super* (or above) natural.

A humanistic motivational talk did not do it. In fact, a similar scenario took Laura's night-terror instantly from being a little girl who had to sleep on her parents' bedroom floor, to being able to sleep at the other end of the house, in her own bedroom, in total darkness (and without curtains at that stage).

When we live according to God's ways, we attract blessing. God will *bless and breathe upon* what is correct. He will *honour and favour* that which is according to His Word and He will *protect* His children from whatever unredeemed life dares to throw at them. In other words, God will leave His supernatural mark or His anointing upon what is according to His way.

THEY STAND OUT

When people position themselves *within* this covering, they breeze through life with minimum disturbance. Sure, there are challenges; sure, there are enemies with a mission to divert and distract, but again, Godly wisdom will always magnificently negotiate people through these.

Who are those who flourish in life, who remain strong and fruitful even in old age (which suggests they were strong and fruitful in their youth)? The answer is those who are *planted in the House of God.* Theirs is a supernatural anointing. Theirs is a supernatural enabling, a supernatural covering and blessing. They live beyond what is natural and normal. They stand out in the crowd or community because they are not subject to this unredeemed environment. Of course they live

Lee and Elijah, 2001

WHEN A CHILD IS BORN,

A FATHER IS BORN.

[FREDERICK BUECHNER]

in it, but they are not *subject* to it. So when they face challenge and opposition, the wisdom they draw upon is not merely 'man's wisdom' – it is Godly wisdom from above that yields answers and breakthrough.

POSITIONED FOR ADVANTAGE

The key to advantage is always in positioning. People being raised in a natural home that loves God will always have an edge on those who don't. Yet an even greater advantage is experienced when that natural home partners with and connects into a great spiritual family or church. The promise of Psalm 92 relates to this.

Allow me to illustrate this from my experience. I was raised in a great natural family. I had wonderful parents and did not lack anything, especially love. Yet at fifteen years of age, my life was still *incomplete* because I had not encountered my Saviour and I had not embraced the wisdom and truth that comes with being planted in the House of God. I will be forever grateful for the foundation my natural parents laid, but I know that the expansiveness of my life today is truly the fruit of many years within the framework of a healthy spiritual House.

A few years ago, a sarcastic criticism found its way back to me. A person had apparently said, "Oh well, I guess I should just be like Bobbie – she just does everything right". When I heard this, my response (okay, my reaction) was, "Hang on! I am NOT Little Miss Perfect! I don't do everything right, but IF I have done anything right, it is that I found Jesus, and at an early age in my Christian walk discovered a love for His House."

If my life is perceived by others to be building into anything substantial, it is simply because my love for this House has *positioned* me well in life. It has positioned me **frequently in His presence** and **frequently under His Word.** These two things alone have the power to build any person's life.

God never intended for any of us to live without these blessings. Even dear people who are isolated and lonely because they have no natural family are taken care of in that God's Word says, "the solitary He has placed in families"(Psalm 68:6). Therefore regardless of our circumstances or natural beginnings, **adoption into the family of God** is rightfully available to EACH AND EVERY-ONE OF US. As far as God is concerned, within the wonderful gift called the family of God, **a warm embrace awaits us all.** Now isn't that a divine thought? Heaven-breathed adoption has the capacity to take anyone who is weak or struggling and change them into something magnificent and supernatural.

Healthy families produce supernaturally charged human beings. How attractive is that in a world hungry for answers and so often only hanging together by a thread?

This dimension of Heaven-on-earth also offers something that the world yearns for, occasionally gets a glimpse of and naively tries to copy. Flick the page and I'll explain.

HEALTHY FAMILIES POSSESS WHAT THE WORLD LONGS FOR

I THINK WE'RE HERE
FOR EACH OTHER

[CAROL BURNETT]

HEALTHY FAMILIES POSSESS WHAT THE WORLD LONGS FOR

LONG — TO HAVE A STRONG WISH OR DESIRE FOR

W hat exactly is this world hungry for? What do people long to experience, apart from health, happiness and enough money to have everyone smiling? Within the very fibre of the human heart, what fundamental needs are common across every country, culture and creed? Psychologists reveal that every human heart yearns for *unconditional love, acceptance* and *a sense of forgiveness* when our humanity lets us down.

I believe **HEALTHY SPIRITUAL FAMILIES have a special ingredient** added to the above, which has the capacity to bind humanity together in a way that would **stun the world**. If the scales fell from people's eyes, this powerful revelation would be the subject matter of every news report and talk-back show. It would find its way to the covers of *Time* and *Newsweek* magazines and would consume front page headlines. Allow me to sow a seed of thought ...

How many of us have ever heard a bunch of young, groovy city business executives say, "Okay, it's Friday night, the weekend is in front of us, let's go out for drinks and *fellowship!*" How many have ever heard a bunch of street thugs say, "Okay, let's go graffiti some city walls and have some *fellowship* in the process!" Will the day ever come when Rachel and Ross (characters of television's popular sitcom 'Friends') are heard to say to Phoebe, Monica and Chandler, "You guys are the best. We just love having *fellowship* with you!"?

No! I don't think so. I doubt that any of us have ever heard it quite put like that.

The word 'fellowship' is not something you hear every day in circles outside the Church. Why is that? Is it because it is classified among what we call 'Christian jargon' or is there another reason?

UNIQUE TO THE KINGDOM

In our ministry I oversee much of the written communications. I try to put my eye across a large percentage of our promotional literature in an attempt to keep our written expression clear, simple and reflective of who we are as a church. One day I found myself looking for a replacement word for 'fellowship.' I can remember thinking, "There has to be a more modern word. Who really relates to this word anyway? It's understood in Church circles, but the unchurched world (whom we are trying to reach) doesn't really relate, plus it just kind of sounds old fashioned."

Well, upon a little investigation I discovered something beautiful about this wonderful 'old-fashioned' word. It is a word totally *unique to the Church*. The word in its original form is 'koinonia.' Now many of you learned Christians reading will be familiar with this. Nonetheless, the meaning unfolds beautifully and carries a dynamic that is relevant to this generation in which we find ourselves living.

Fellowship literally means '*sharing, unity, close association, participation and partnership.*' Aren't these words great, but it gets better! (But wait! There's more! and it's not steak knives☺). The Strong's Bible Dictionary defines it this way –"It is a **cementing together** of God's people and it is something that is **only brought about by the Holy Spirit**."

In other words, the full impact, the full dynamic, the full package of living a life where one can experience all the blessing and benefit of a sense of *sharing, unity, close association, participation and partnership* is only attainable and only available in an environment where the Holy Spirit is known. Now I pray that you are hearing the full impact of this.

There are many environments, both within the Church and outside, where *aspects* of these qualities exist, but the *full package*, the *full expression* of them is only found in those places where the Holy Spirit is loved, embraced, responded to and obeyed. I'm sure you will agree that outside of the Kingdom, people don't generally love and acknowledge the Holy Spirit – so while their clubs, pubs and various groups might be enjoyable, fun and somewhat fulfilling, the full impact of being cemented together in this Heaven-inspired unity and partnership will never be fully experienced.

In many Christian circles we see elements of the above, yet so many environments *fall short of achieving their full potential* of true fellowship, because they don't understand or embrace the dynamics of the Spirit. In some places this is by choice and in others it is because of a lack of understanding. Yet let me say it again, the full impact of being **cemented together** will never be totally realised.

NOT EASILY SHAKEN

So what's the point? The human spirit, regardless of whether it is redeemed or not, is wired in such a way that it either consciously or subconsciously yearns to be connected with this **depth of relationship, friendship and value** – a sense of belonging that in reality is *not easily shaken.*

This is where believers inside the Church often fail to recognise and value the magnificent gift that is SITTING IN THEIR VERY LAPS. Secular sporting clubs, social groups, or even noble welfare organisations may engage in and enjoy aspects of this wonder, but sadly when offence or opposition challenges their relationships (or even their cause) they don't have the 'cementing ingredient' (the Holy Spirit) that enables them to **overcome and endure.**

Fellowship is the capacity to be **firmly united** in a cause bigger than yourself. Fellowship is the capacity of being able **to share common ground without conflict.** Fellowship is the capacity of **participating** in a **partnership** that is **held or cemented together** by a force that originates from another dimension and world (ie: Heaven). Sounds almost too perfect to be true, yet it is a crucial key in seeing God's Kingdom established down here on earth.

ENDURING

The awesome Holy Spirit has been given to us from Heaven to facilitate all of this. The Father gave Him the job profile of coming alongside and helping us each reach our potential. Outside of supernatural intervention, influence and principles, it is actually very difficult for people to remain connected for their entire lifetime, or the length of the course.

At Hillsong Church, the vast majority of our key people have been with us long term. This means we have each seen the good, the bad and the ugly of our individual seasons and growth curves. What holds us together? The glue is God's dear and awesome Holy Spirit. As the Bible teaches us, He is the One who reveals the truth in God's Word, which then **enables liberty and growth across our relationships.** Just the whisper of His presence **brings creativity and power beyond our human ability**; and above and beyond anything else, He reveals CHRIST, who in turn reveals to us the Father, whose very being *connects us to a Cause greater than ourselves.*

Quite honestly, I think the average person doing-life-on-the-planet, if presented with the reality of this gift, would find it hard to resist. Who in their right mind would say, "No thank you, I'd rather struggle along in my own strength"?

Therefore our challenge as believers is to *present* the House of God in a way that embraces the fullness of the gift given to us in the Person of the Holy Spirit. Creating this atmosphere across our everyday lives and in a way that is not *religious* or *'weird'* becomes something too attractive to resist or reject. Our responsibility as believers is to make this treasure accessible to a lost world longing for reality, and none of us can bring this dynamic to others until it first becomes reality for us personally.

We have talked so far about our lives being enhanced by the supernatural magnificence of Heaven. Allow the analogy to now become even more practical because I believe that healthy families have mastered the art of simply doing certain things together.

CHAPTER SIX

HEALTHY FAMILIES EAT TOGETHER

HEALTHY FAMILIES EAT TOGETHER

Dear friend, I trust you are beginning to catch a greater revelation of the dynamic that represents the House of God. I respect the fact that many of you reading this are great men and women of God, with an intelligent understanding of His ways. However, I hope you agree that God can take any truth and 'tweak our understanding,' 'turn the lights on' or cause the 'penny to drop even more.' Then what we may have known for years suddenly takes on a whole new clarity and understanding. We are living in and entering days when the simple truths that bear the most fruit will become brighter, more refined and more obvious. As Proverbs 4:18 says, "The path of the just shines brighter and brighter unto the perfect day."

For some reason the reality of **spiritual family within the House of God** is one such truth. I stand in amazement that so many don't see it. They are born again, Heaven-bound and yet they reduce God's Kingdom to almost an *addendum* to their lives. They limit this family to a casual affair instead of a passionate first-love affair, and then wonder why they aren't as happy and prosperous as the Word declares they should be. Even beautiful, devoted and loyal 'lovers of God' can miss the point, and I've heard such people say, "I love God, I live my life for the Kingdom, but today my understanding has grown." With that, a greater dimension of love and appreciation for the people in their 'God-world,' their 'God-family,' and 'their church' has emerged.

The people God connects us to in His Kingdom are not *mere acquaintances* who serve a less than eternal purpose or worse still, selfish motive. They are family – God's sons and daughters, our brothers and sisters who just happen to be alongside us in the portion of history that we are walking through together. Understanding this *changes your entire perspective.*

I'll expand on this later but suddenly, 'visitors' for example, are not an intrusion to our parking space or favourite seat – they are seen as perhaps *long lost family* God has been waiting to reunite us with. Suddenly, the 'weekly sermon' cannot be missed because it is Heaven's nourishment – our daily bread needful for health and direction. Suddenly, 'newborn Christians' joyfully engage *everyone's* attention because "Hey, there are new babies in the House." (One of the great disappointments in church life is seeing selfish or thoughtless believers packing up and heading for the car park as a Salvation call is being made). Suddenly, even 'the slightly simple people' draw forth more embracing tolerance, because they are simply our Father's precious ones. Jesus said, "The poor (or frail or simple) we would have with us always" (Matthew 26:11).

CENTRAL TO HEALTH

Suddenly it all changes, because the House is no longer a *centre* that Christians casually visit, but it becomes "our family", and it is *central* to not only our health, but also the health of the community and society in which God has so strategically placed us (and for which He will also one day hold us accountable).

For that reason (and I believe it's a very good reason) healthy families just do certain things together. No option, no debate, no theological argument needed on this one. The analogy is 'natural' and the principle applies powerfully in the 'spiritual'.

Healthy families, for example, eat together!

Okay… let's think about food for a moment. First of all, food is *good*! It is *desirable* and *essential*! A lack of food has been known to make people a little irritable around the edges! So we all agree food is good. Jesus didn't throw in that little sentence "Give us this day our daily bread" for poetic licence.

Natural food is essential and spiritual food is even more essential, and I am sure that no one reading this will argue this point. I believe a healthy family is marked by its ability to break both natural and spiritual bread together. In life there is nothing more delightful than watching a bunch of people enjoying a good meal around a big old table - fine food, fine beverage, fine atmosphere! Conversation, laughter, connection and a sense of contentment in having shared something good together.

Various cultures around this wonderful world of ours could teach us so much. The Italian culture by nature is magnificent at *doing food!* – Italian families know how to eat. Their culture embraces every age – from toddlers with cheeks that have been so kissed and pinched that they are permanently pink, through to much loved grandparents, whose wisdom and age are greatly honoured. The food comes out in abundance; and there is always more than enough because visitors and friends, and even strangers are almost expected. Such is the 'over and above' that everyone goes home, arms laden with fresh goodies for others to enjoy. (Okay, who feels the sudden need to rush out and purchase an airline ticket to Italia?)

GROWING STRONG

I don't want to exhaust the analogy (actually, I do) but this is how the House of God should be. Italians love 'company.' Dissect the word into its original Latin and you have 'com' which means *together*, and 'pani' which means *bread*. (I actually read this in a European car magazine in an article about Italy☺.) *'Com-pani'* is the ability to come together, eat great food and grow stronger both naturally and spiritually.

Believers also come together each week and break bread. We gather with expectant hearts, eager to have the Bread of Life, the Word of God, and God's manna spread before us. We should embrace it like our lives depended upon it. Does this mean our own personal and private reading is invalid? Of course not, but Jesus did give us a *pattern for effective living* and the tenor of scripture is to *not neglect to gather together* (Hebrews 10:25). He himself broke bread, drank wine, shared hope and encouragement, and told His disciples to do likewise as often as they wished.

Let's also not reduce 'communion' to a mere *church service tradition* of taking a little cup and a morsel of bread. Communion, which lovingly calls to remembrance our Saviour's sacrifice, is very powerful and something we should always embrace, but our 'communion' is more expansive than this alone. It should also be the way **we love and embrace the teaching of His Word** as brought to us by the shepherds, pastors and leaders God has placed in and over our lives.

Churches that neglect to feed their people great spiritual food become unhealthy.

THEIR MEAT IS TO
'DO THE WILL OF THE FATHER'

[JOHN 5:30]

Churches that serve up the Word in meagre rations become malnourished, and churches that serve up the Word with no love, no warmth and no sense of effort barely keep their congregations alive.

I believe that communion **also embraces our ability to simply hang out and enjoy each other's company** – and who agrees that there is no better place to do that than over a great meal? If ever we have the luxury of opening a restaurant in our church complex, I would love to call it 'Table for Twelve.' I can just imagine Jesus walking into the restaurants of His day and being heard to order, "Table for twelve, thanks! (... and roll up an extra chair for the thirteenth)."

CONNECTING PEOPLE

I honestly believe that food is an integral part of the Kingdom and should be a magnificent part of God's House. (My heart is honestly not to offend, but when did an insipid cup of cheap, instant coffee and a dry cookie ever reflect the excellence of Heaven?)

Friends, family and faith that neglect any of the above, build a deficit into their relationships. On that note, Hillsong Church may not be perfect (in fact, it isn't), but the overwhelming response we often hear from new people attending is, "You teach the Word in such a way that we can go home and immediately apply or eat it."

As our churches increase in size, I think we all need to *discover clever ways of connecting people.* We have a philosophy at Hillsong Church that says, "as the church gets larger, it also needs to get smaller." This realisation emcompasses our CELL STRUCTURE, where we want to see every person connected in a small group designed to accomplish all that we've been talking about so far.

Our earnest desire is to see countless small groups scattered across our city, full of people who know how to hang out, enjoy, and among other things, eat together (both naturally and spiritually) in such a way that *fellowship is nourished.* I pray that they will all be open-hearted enough to always have an open door and a place set at the table (or whatever) for invited or unexpected visitors. As in the days of old, they broke bread from house to house and our magnificent Lord added daily such as should be saved (Acts 2:46,47).

Such is the nature of a healthy natural family and such is the nature of a healthy spiritual church. Hey, I think one of the first things we are going to do in Heaven is trade our Sunday best for something comfy (comfortable) and eternal and then sit down to a giant meal together. May as well start practising now, which for some may prove challenging. (Some will need to break out of their comfort zone, go beyond the negatives that contain them when it comes to human relations, and simply get to know the other fabulous people that God has chosen to plant them alongside).

Healthy families are also exceptional at playing together...

CHAPTER SEVEN

HEALTHY FAMILIES PLAY TOGETHER

NEVER FORGET HOW TO PLAY

CHAPTER SEVEN

HEALTHY FAMILIES PLAY TOGETHER

PLAY — TO AMUSE ONESELF PLEASANTLY
WITH FREEDOM OF MOVEMENT

A few years ago, I remember reading an article in a reputable newspaper about various near death experiences. One woman recounted dying and feeling herself drawn towards ... 'whatever.' As she got nearer, she heard the sounds of LAUGHTER AND HAPPINESS. Her shocked response was, "Oh no! God has a sense of humour!" Now to be honest, the validity of that story is not the issue, but the reality remains – Heaven IS a happy, joyful and without doubt GREAT PLACE to be *and we're called to bring this atmosphere and dynamic to earth.*

Walk into some churches that bear His beautiful name above the door and it is more like walking into a funeral parlour than into a-touch-of-Heaven-on-earth. This may seem harsh and the last thing I want to do is offend, but there are some places where some believers need to pop outside, get some fresh air, sunshine and blood moving through their veins and realise that their appearance and conservatism really isn't reflecting well on their amazing God. It is worth noting that 'conservative' actually means 'resistant to change.' We all need to be mindful of extremes, but sometimes being resistant to change has kept pockets of the Church locked in the Dark Ages.

Child-likeness is big on God's agenda. I'm not talking about immaturity, but child-likeness. The ability to view life with *wide-eyed wonder*, the ability to never lose *a contagious sense of playfulness* and the ability to not *take oneself (or life for that matter) too seriously*. I believe that the *child in us* never dies, despite age or responsibility. We will always and forever be His kids and our churches would be much happier places if all of us never forget that.

LOOSE THE CONTAINMENT

Healthy natural families and healthy spiritual families have that 'special something' about them, that creates an atmosphere where anything could happen and usually does. They are **spontaneous** and **free-spirited** environments where people are encouraged to enjoy their Creator, life and one another (however not at the risk of being disrespectful, strange or weird). To be brutally honest – our churches would be **far more attractive to the world we desire to reach** if we lost the 'prune-faced starchiness' and simply learnt how to be ourselves, with a little *personality* thrown in for good measure.

Let me divert for a moment. On the subject of personality…we ALL have a personality. Some people actually need to hear this. God did not grace some with personality and others not. All of us (not just the bold and the beautiful who can hold the attention of a room) are wonderfully endowed with personality, because we are ALL created in the image of a wonderful God who is actually full of personality.

I personally believe that God has a sense of humour and must be extremely fun to be around, because you only have to look at some of His offspring – they're hilarious! The sad reality for some is that often a negative or less than joyful upbringing can cloud that wonderful personality into something less than it was intended to be. It is for this reason we all need to allow the awesome transforming Word of God, and the many and varied works of the Holy Spirit to **remove our CONTAINMENT so that our true delightful self can emerge**.

I heard my husband once say, "Children did not *flock around Jesus* for *compulsory religious instruction*. They ran after Him because He was awesome to be around." Perhaps He was to children what honey is to bees and perhaps that is a great way for you and me to assess our effectiveness as Christians. What is it that attracts or repels the people we are trying to reach?

LAUGHTER IS GOOD FOR US

Back to the subject – **Healthy families play together**. They take time to enjoy and CONNECT and grow wonderfully close in the process. This doesn't mean we do not take the task at hand seriously. We have a lost world to reach and minister to, but laughter is without doubt medicine to the soul (Proverbs 17:22). We also live in a world that generally thinks that Christianity is anything but fun, spontaneous and enjoyable.

At Hillsong Church I feel so very, very, very blessed to be surrounded with the kind of people I've been writing about. Even when we as a church face challenging periods, we seriously never lose our ability to laugh and enjoy one another. I know that it is actually a powerful and liberating strength and that there is nothing more irritating to the enemy than an advancing battle-line of seriously happy and rejoicing Christians.

I remember one Sunday evening my husband wanted me to share as we received the offering. Brian introduced me, saying "This is my wife, Roberta Lee Houston" (as if the church didn't already know) and then he began to rave on: "This is my wife, my only wife, my beautiful wife, the wife of my youth ... (rave, rave, rave)." And then, in front of a crowd of 1,500 people, he grabbed me, threw me back and planted the biggest pash (as in KISS) on my mouth. I am not exaggerating – this was one of those full-on, in-your-face moments, where we were doing circles around the stage. I didn't know what to do – get into it, or hit him so he'd stop. I chose the latter! After about ONE MINUTE (hello!) I surfaced. The church went crazy. They were whistling, whooping and rolling on the floor laughing. As I tried to rearrange my hair and relocate my lipstick (which was now on Brian's face), he sat down and left me to the offering. How does one do the offering without lipstick? Then to make it even funnier, some quick thinking person yelled out, "I'll have what she's having!" (which just happens to be the title of my first book).

Now, I don't recommend you preachers try that, and we certainly didn't try it in the next of our multiple services. It was a **spontaneous moment** in the life of our church that brought a wonderful **sense of family** into the place. "Hey! Pastor Brian and Bobbie may be over forty, but they still love each other, hee hee hee!" That crazy moment brought more than life and hilarity into the place, it brought a *sense of security* ... and it still makes me smile.

ENRICHED

I realise all families are unique and different, but the reality is, God created us with this diversity and this is where 'church life' can be so exciting and so totally irresistible. By being part of the BIG GOD FAMILY, **our lives are enriched by exposure to fabulous people from beyond our immediate little world,** and this is what makes the Kingdom so delightfully colourful and wonderful.

How sad and boring to go through life and only ever get close to a handful of people. If the perfect will of God for your world is literally only a small network of people, then I am not devaluing that, but I know God has created the majority of us for a far more expansive world than we often realise.

Growing up I had two parents and one sister. (I desperately wanted a dog, but wasn't allowed one.) I also had a handful of relatives whom I saw once or twice a year, and a handful of friends at school. Now admittedly I was young and had not entered an adult environment, but nonetheless where I am going with this point remains. I then got saved. The light went on, the curtains were drawn back and the sun arose upon a whole new world. Today, because of God's great grace, we have a circle of friends and family who embrace literally thousands around the world and who add a **richness that is beyond comprehension**. To outsiders observing this could be regarded as a rare treasure, yet it is a gift available to *every person and every church* across the planet. The only restrictions are the boundaries we set ourselves.

How lovely that culture, denomination and age are no longer restrictive to those hungry for truth. More than at any other time in history, people are crossing traditional boundaries and are gathering to the Cause of Jesus Christ and because of that God's Kingdom is experiencing a new found freedom.

The bottom line is that life is too short and too precious to do without the freedom of laughter, joy and playfulness. I pray that in the midst of this stage called Life, we can all discover how to make the journey *enjoyable, memorable and fun* for those alongside. How lovely if those who ascribe to His greatness could literally become a memorable experience for everyone they encounter. Begin to live like this and we might begin to truly catch a glimpse of Heaven on earth!

Decide to spend your life with this family and you will also discover yourself 'growing together'…

Joel Houston, 22, and 'Buddy' Houston, 8 weeks

FRIENDS, FAMILY, FAITH ... AND A
PUPPY ON MY HEAD

CHAPTER EIGHT

HEALTHY FAMILIES GROW TOGETHER

Reuben Morgan and Marty Sampson

YOU CAN'T BE HUMAN ALONE

[MARGARET KUHN]

CHAPTER EIGHT

HEALTHY FAMILIES GROW TOGETHER

GROW – TO SPRING UP, DEVELOP AND MATURE

Healthy families grow together. In other words, they are **prepared to do the seasons of life together.** At the beginning of this book I shared my hope regarding life – "That I might love the Lord my God with all my heart, soul and strength - that the people in my world would also love this same God with all their heart, soul and strength – and that when the rewards are being handed out in Heaven, not one precious person will be missing."

To achieve this requires a commitment to the people around you that says, "Hey! I am prepared to do life with you. In fact, I'm not just prepared, **I WOULD LOVE TO DO LIFE WITH YOU.**" It is a commitment which takes the good and the bad of one another's journey and chooses to emerge on the other side together, intact and with nobody missing.

I will forever treasure a 'planning roster' that our friend and worship pastor Darlene once sent me regarding a conference we were organising. Handwritten on the bottom were the words, "I count it an honour to love God with you, love Darls." When we learn to verbalise these simple heartfelt moments, it adds a dimension to life that IS eternal.

The commitment to do life together is the defining framework of a great natural family, but sadly so many in our world are missing out on this gold because they have lost the ability to *endure the tough times*. **The moment they are challenged they forfeit, bail out, abdicate and tragically rob themselves** of the joy of growing into places of victory and success together.

At the time of penning this chapter, our church is twenty-four years old. In that time there are a number of us who have done a whole lot of growing together. Our founders Frank and Hazel Houston may have been in their mid-fifties when they decided to uproot from New Zealand and follow God's direction to plant another church in Sydney, but the majority of us were really a bunch of kids. I stand with thousands who honour Frank and Hazel for that **brave step of obedience**. When many their age were preparing for retirement, they were casting earthly care to the wind and were catching a bus to the first meeting of what now, many years later, constitutes the Hillsong Church. By the way, that first meeting had nine people so never despise the day of small beginnings. Anything substantial in God always begins as a seed.

LONGEVITY

Well, that bunch of kids has grown into a company of adults and we are still pressing on with so many who have been with us from the beginning. Of course a few have come and gone , yet the reality is that our leadership team has been together a long time now.

Why is our church marked with this longevity? I present the question because longevity is not as common for many churches as you would expect it to be. I have heard a sad statistic that revealed that the average pastor in America only stays with his congregation for five years. FIVE YEARS! This is actually alarming because we are talking about **the shepherd** here. No wonder the enemy delights in delaying progress in so many places. This attitude or mindset means that not many are staying long enough to establish anything substantial.

Psalm 92 describes those who remain strong and fruitful, even into old age. These are the ones who allow their roots to go down. They do not uproot every five minutes or five years for that matter. Instead they allow themselves to become planted. I am not discrediting a day and age where people move and often face frequent job transfers for example, but I am drawing attention to a fickle attitude among believers which has them *all too quickly* uprooting with no consideration of consequence to them, their children, the future generations or even the spiritual family they might be leaving.

RIGHT REASONS

Let's go back to the analogy of a healthy family that has been brought together by God. They will PRODUCE CHILDREN who will grow up and eventually move out to establish their own life, but **their move will always be for all the right reasons**. It will not be an incorrect disconnection or worse still, a severing of relationship which sadly is all too common. I think there is nothing more disheartening to the Father and more disruptive to the Kingdom of God than the fragmentation of "spiritual family." This really is an issue the Church needs to address if we are going to come anywhere close to bringing Heaven to earth in this generation.

One day our three children will all grow up, find their feet, no doubt fall in love, marry and leave 'our house.' For Brian and me it will be a bitter/sweet day, but hopefully THEY WILL NEVER LEAVE US. Hopefully we will always be in their lives. Hopefully we will always hold a treasured place in their hearts and will always stay connected. Why? BECAUSE WE ARE FAMILY (plus I'd totally throttle them if they entertained anything less than the above). As I said previously, when we arrive in Heaven, I want to make a very loud *blow-the-trumpet-and-get-everybody's-attention* announcement about the two most important families in my life. I seriously want to be able to say - 'The Houstons' and 'the Hillsong Church' have arrived! Everyone is here – the kids, their families, their children, their world of influence, the whole lot, we are ALL here! Lord, you put us together, we grew, we were faithful and here we are – **full of life, full of experience, full of stories to tell - Abba Father, BRING ON THE PARTY!"**

Healthy families, both natural and spiritual would not trade the above for anything. No offence, no tragedy, no circumstance be it negative or positive, in fact nothing in Heaven or earth will separate them from this prize to be obtained both individually and corporately. I pray that all of our churches may become stronger in this arena of life.

Dysfunction is usually the result of ignorance, intolerance and lack of Godly wisdom. The Bible so wisely says, "Train up a child in the way they should go and they will not quickly depart." *Training is a lifetime commitment* that isn't quickly discarded when we hit the first (or second or third) challenge, and it doesn't quickly succumb to disillusionment because the process is taking a little longer than anticipated.

Healthy families are marked by their God-breathed ability to walk hand in hand through the many and varied seasons of life – they're prepared to negotiate the good, the bad and even the ugly of life.

To enjoy all this benefit and wonder, healthy families also realise how essential it is to know how to support one another through the good and difficult times.

CHAPTER NINE

HEALTHY FAMILIES SUPPORT EACH OTHER

'HER VALUE ...

BEYOND RUBIES '
OR PEARLS

[PROVERBS 31:10]

HEALTHY FAMILIES SUPPORT
EACH OTHER

SUPPORT — TO KEEP FROM FALLING OR FAILURE, TO GIVE HELP AND
COUNTENANCE TO

Unconditional love and acceptance! That is what I felt the Spirit of God say when He described His people as 'family.' Unconditional love and acceptance throws a whole new spotlight on the negatives of human nature. Now I'm sure many will agree that human nature is prone to behaviour that is often less than attractive. We have all at some time been subjected to (or even been guilty of) irritability, over-sensitivity, misunderstanding, disagreement, offence, hurt, or even injustice.

Unconditional love and acceptance is therefore *'the welcome home cushion,'* *'the safety net'* and *'the arm of correction'* of family. It is *'the haven of warmth'* that beckons us when that big bad world has been mean or unkind. It even resembles *big fleshy arms that wrap themselves around us* when forgiveness is needed and embrace is seemingly undeserved.

Unconditional love and acceptance paints a picture of support in the good times and the bad times. When people are excelling, we cheer; when people are rejoicing, we rejoice also; when they prosper, we smile and applaud. It sounds perfect in theory, yet it is amazing how many struggle with these. And of course when life is not turning out as expected, when life appears unfair, we are also right there to help.

Unconditional love and acceptance is at the very core of God. Unconditional love and acceptance should therefore exude from every corner of His House. Let me say that again – every corner! It should be felt the moment people enter our doors, and then be experienced in every department and across every level of ministry and leadership.

If this was the case, it would separate the House of God from every other organisation on the planet. It would mark the House of God with a uniqueness, a quality and a power that would *release and empower the human spirit to excel*. None of us enjoys the negatives of life, we all bruise easily and we all need to be nourished and built up with encouragement. Healthy natural families and healthy spiritual families realise and aim for this.

LOVING PEOPLE

I mentioned earlier a profound comment one of our pastors made. She said, "Nobody needs to leave this church. Why would anyone leave a functional family?" For our churches to become these functional families we need to learn how to *negotiate wisely* both the wonderful and the less-than-wonderful seasons of life.

Church life above and before all else, is about people, and *people doing life* encounter all sorts of challenges. When the challenge is on, every church needs to become stronger at *recognising, locating and then helping* such people. As much as a healthy natural family would not stand by and passively (or helplessly) allow one of its beloved members to suffer, neither should our churches.

We have an ongoing challenge to train ourselves and others to be alert to needs and then put in place the ministries and programs to effectively cater for these needs. If we all engaged this better, our Christianity would not fall short at "word only", but would be felt powerfully "in deed" also (Acts 10:38; Col 3:16,17).

It is then that Heaven's love and Heaven's acceptance would be felt down here. **Heaven would be in the House** and the House would then effectively touch society. Instead of the temptation to judge or point the finger, there would be an overwhelming compulsion to lend a helping hand. Instead of offence or misunderstanding yielding isolation, we would choose to understand human frailty, forgive and extend a shoulder to lean upon. Rather than only plan and cater selfishly to our immediate sphere, we would approach life intelligently and endeavour to put strategies in place to cater for all the challenges that this generation faces. The Word says of King David, "He served his generation well"(Acts 13:36). To the best of his ability he understood the needs of his own generation and met them, but he also lived knowing and preparing for the generations that would follow.

We have several thousand people in our church (and growing), so life is full of wonderful stories and testimonies, but one of the most exciting things of late is that we are hearing more and more stories of 'outsiders' (non-Hillsong Church people) telling other non-Hillsong Church people that they should go down to "that church" because the people down there will help you. Isn't that simply the best! The unchurched world recognising that "**the House down there" is prepared, equipped and willing to help**. I personally think that is the ultimate compliment and prize. It delights our heart, yet how much more our King in Heaven, who is anxious to rescue hurting humanity.

THINKING GENERATIONALLY

May we all, as believers and leaders alike in the Kingdom today, live our lives with this wonderful mark of stewardship. I love and admire my husband because his 'leadership anointing' stretches well into the future. While very mindful of the present, his *view* embraces the future strategically and we will not only serve our own generation well, but we will (by the grace of God) pass the baton on *very effectively* to the next.

For example, our House resounds with a youth generation who write songs and worship God because Brian and our leadership team made a conscious decision to draw the youth into this arena of church life many years ago. Because of that a youth culture has emerged who know how to give expression to their passion. If you are a pastor or leader, then may I encourage you to not *age your church prematurely* by failing to bring through the young people. So many churches sabotage their future by failing to keep *their platform (of influence)* young and youthful. A healthy House or church embraces all the generations. (For that reason I hope you love the attached CD.)

In bringing Part One of this book to closure, I strongly believe that God in His infinite wisdom has provided us with **a treasure to be found in family**. Only an insane world would take a newborn baby, thrust it into the cold streets and wish it 'good luck' in its survival. No! Baby boys and baby girls are birthed into the loving embrace of family – and for *an entire lifetime*.

In the same way, **newborn sons and daughters of God FLOURISH** when they find and embrace the spiritual family that God intends them to be planted in. Again it is bordering on insanity to lead a person to Jesus, thrust a Bible in their hand and then expect them to excel in becoming a radical disciple of Christ by themselves. We need each other. We need to be surrounded by awesome men and women, and 'spiritual' mums and dads, and brothers and sisters if we are going to truly thrive in the ways and goodness of God. The responsibility is ours to discover. I am not responsible for yours and you are not responsible for mine, but together we can create a world where to do so is not a futile treasure hunt.

If you are not 'planted' or you are confused, then allow yourself to be honest and real, and talk to your Heavenly Father about this. I am confident that with an issue as important as this He would not keep a mystery from you.

For those of you in leadership like ourselves, then let's truly realise that **our leadership responsibility is to create this environment**. That we might take our places of worship and turn them into THE most magnificent families on earth – warm, embracing, connective, fun, nurturing and productive. Healthy families do produce magnificent people.

As mentioned in the beginning, I felt the Lord say two more things, "I also call you a Body and a House." Let's see what the pen will deliver regarding these two wonderful analogies.

ESSENTIALS
FOR A HEALTHY FAMILY

- REMEMBER WE ARE ALL ON A JOURNEY OF DISCOVERY

- BE PATIENT WITH THE LEARNING CURVES OF OTHERS

- VERBALISE LOVE FREQUENTLY

- SMILE AND GIVE YOUR FACE A REST

- FORGIVE EASILY

- LET THE WORDS "I LOVE YOU" BE THE ONLY WORDS OVER WHICH THE SUN SETS

- GIVE WRITTEN EXPRESSION TO LOVE WITH ENCOURAGING LETTERS AND CARDS WHICH ENDURE THE YEARS

- REACH OUT, TOUCH AND EMBRACE OFTEN

- PROTECT AND NURTURE WHAT IS IMPORTANT

- DON'T HAVE A NERVOUS BREAKDOWN OVER WHAT IS NOT IMPORTANT

- DON'T SWEAT THE SMALL STUFF

- CULTIVATE SPONTANEITY

- LAUGH OFTEN

- WHEN IT IS WITHIN YOUR POWER, GIVE!

- WHEN YOU LEARN, TEACH

- CELEBRATE THE MOMENTS THAT COUNT

- MEASURE EVERYTHING ON THE SCALE OF ETERNITY!

PART TWO

'I CALL YOU A BODY!'

BODY — A GROUP OF PERSONS
REGARDED COLLECTIVELY

CHAPTER TEN

HEALTHY BODIES REALISE
THEY ARE A BODY

CONNECT
AND SURPRISE YOURSELF

HEALTHY BODIES REALISE
THEY ARE A BODY

REALISE – TO CONCEIVE AS REAL AND CONVERT INTO REALITY

———

The Body of Christ – the term has been around for centuries and will evoke various responses. For some, it will raise fond thoughts; for others there will be no response at all; and for still others it may inflame an undesirable feeling in the pit of their stomach. Why is this? Possibly because the term encapsulates an image of a company of people who call themselves believers and whose responses or behaviour have the capacity to powerfully colour another's perception and impression. We often remind our church that people outside the Kingdom (and inside for that matter) are judging Christ, our church and even Brian and myself on their behaviour.

Across the planet, the Body of Christ comes in all shapes and sizes. Some are large, some are small, some are strong and some are weaker. Some carry themselves with kind affection and some appear to show no affection at all. Just as the Word says in Matthew 12:34, "Out of the fullness (the overflow, the super-abundance) of the heart the mouths speaks," the same can be said of these various church bodies that populate the earth. Out of the **health or ill-health** of their collective corporate heart their various mouths give voice and according to what comes forth, it can equal a pleasant or unpleasant experience for those who encounter it.

I personally believe the Body of Christ is designed to be magnificent, and as is the theme of this book the analogy relates to Heaven effectively finding its way into our world. To believers who are keen to *live effective, powerful, productive lives* this is a captivating thought, but to believers who are content or complacent to be passive, they might feel tempted to skip the next few pages (but I hope they won't).

Okay, so here's the deal – healthy bodies realise they are a Body. They understand that they are not a collection of unrelated and unconnected limbs, 'doing their own thing.' The image of a collection of unconnected body bits is bizarre and amusing, yet it is reflective of far too many churches, who then ponder in bewilderment why they are not being as effective as they would wish.

Ephesians 4 describes a scene that has Heaven in party mode and everyone down here deliriously happy and prosperous:

> "Rather, let our lives lovingly express **truth** [in all things, speaking truly, dealing truly, living truly]. Enfolded in love, let us grow up in every way and in all things into Him Who is the Head, [even] Christ (the Messiah, the Anointed One).
> For because of Him **the whole body (the church, in all its various parts)**, closely joined and firmly knit together by the joints and ligaments with which it is supplied, when each part [with power adapted to its need] is working properly [in all its functions], **grows to full maturity, building itself up in love"**. [Ephesians 4:15,16 AMP]

These verses are implying that if all the limbs and ligaments, and bits and pieces decided to *get along*, decided to *function according to their design*, decided to *contribute*, decided to *never rebel or become independent in attitude*, decided never to be *jealous or envious*, decided never to *wilfully dislocate themselves*… then the Body would grow, increase and prosper, and Heaven also would rejoice because it would be all the richer for the effort. All we have to do is realise and appreciate we are such a Body and then act accordingly.

CONNECTED

CONNECTION is a powerful concept and a word that is becoming quite vogue across the landscape of the church today. Is it merely another trendy church growth concept, or is it an eternal principle? I think it is the latter.

God did not use the analogy of the body because He was lost for concepts. The intricacies and wonder of the human body are fruit of our Creator's very fertile mind. **To then liken His Church and precious Bride collectively to a body is also part of His genius** and we might all prosper in our endeavours if we were to not to underestimate this living, breathing, walking illustration.

Friend, if we were to get personal, where are you located in the Body that is your place of worship right now? If God pulled out a big blackboard and drew a picture of your church with arms and legs, torso and head, and then labelled it with individual's names, where would we find your name? Would your label represent a visible part or an unseen part? Hopefully it would not represent a 'position vacant spot.' Agree with me or not, but this is a very challenging thought.

Healthy churches and healthy individual Christians are 'healthy' because they have grasped this revelation. The *corporate call* is that together this Body would stand tall and strong in society. She should be agile, fit, equipped and able to meet the needs of the community in which she is planted. When outsiders observe this Body in action, they should be *impressed*. They should stop in their tracks and be heard to say (or at least think), "What an incredible specimen. That Body reflects well on her Creator."

The human body is only as effective as its *collective health*. God likens life and us (individually and corporately) to magnificent athletes. One dislocated, inflamed or unco-operative limb can seriously limit potential, and any athlete will tell you how frustrating it is to have their dreams dashed because of one *damaged or difficult limb*.

In the same way, we as individual limbs and ligaments in the Body can **enhance or limit God's purposes across the earth**. Brian and I have a dream and aspiration that the Hillsong Church will be a magnificent reflection of her Maker. We desire for her to run well in life, to achieve her created purpose and to cross the finish line and secure all the promises and prizes that rightfully belong to her. We live to bring Heaven to earth in our particular sphere of influence, and because Brian and I are evenly yoked in this calling, we are together the spiritual head. Alongside our vision and eldership team, **the heart and soul of our church is fashioned and determined by our leadership**.

We are responsible to have *eyes to see* what God wants us to see, we are responsible to have *ears to hear* what God wants us to hear, and we are responsible to *communicate what is in His heart*. If we as this spiritual head become 'brain dead' (now there's a thought) then the Body we are attached to will be seriously impaired. From this anointed and authoritative position, Brian and I are also

PEN AND INK STUDY OF PROPORTIONS
FROM VITRUVIUS'S DE ARCHITECTURA
[LEONARDO DA VINCI, ACCADEMIA, VENICE]

responsible for sending clear, uncluttered messages to the rest of the Body, which then *mobilises that Body to action.*

As beautiful as each part of the Body is, without these clear avenues of communication that same Body would behave and carry herself in a very disjointed, unattractive and more than likely ineffective way. WE DESPERATELY NEED EACH OTHER.

EFFECTIVE

Friend, it is not enough to be merely saved and Heaven bound. 1 Timothy 1:9 declares that we are "saved and called." In a nutshell - at Salvation we find ourselves *rescued*, which is simply too amazing for words. The *redemptive process begins* and hopefully as we co-operate with the Word and the Spirit, our lives begin on the *process of restoration.*

Yet God never intended it to end there. Redemption's plan is to bring us to health and restoration, so that we might then *rule* and *reign* in life, so that 'together and called' we can stand and **effectively represent Heaven.** In doing so we bring His will to bear on this world around us. Saved and called! As my husband so brilliantly states, "too many Christians only live saved." To facilitate Heaven's heartbeat, we all need to live SAVED AND CALLED – and trust me, the world would be a better place.

How amazing to realise our lives *collectively* can accomplish so much. Yet the penetrating question is, 'What are we called to accomplish?' If all the many and varied and extensive 'good works' of the church could be articulated into one sentence, how would that sentence read? Is there one sentence that can encapsulate the mission of the Church? One sentence that can embrace vision, expansion, care, teaching and evangelism? Well, I believe that **She, the Church of the living God, has been called to carry the very heartbeat of God the Father to a lost, lonely, often isolated and dying world.** And I believe that as a functioning healthy Body, with her heart beating in time with His, She is not only **commissioned** but She is also powerfully *enabled* and *empowered* to cause this world to not only sit up and listen, but hopefully also to respond.

How divine and sobering - our heart beating in perfect time with His!

I recently found a beautiful coffee-table book entitled *Family* that in essence celebrates the magnificence of humanity. Of course my heart did leaps and bounds and I momentarily got frustrated that I didn't have access (as they did) to 17,000 photographers and 40,000 photos – nevertheless one giant spread revealed a collage of faces with a caption that said, "all beating with one heart."

Our world frequently celebrates the magnitude and magnificence of creation, but so often it fails to recognise the Creator behind the Creation. As believers we have an awesome opportunity to present the Truth, the Answer, the Reason for our existence to those around. *Don't sabotage that moment with behaviour that contradicts the Body we represent.* The beautiful people we encounter who are hungering for truth and reality deserve more than that.

HUMANITY CRIES
AND ONE HEART RESPONDS

CHAPTER ELEVEN

HEALTHY BODIES CARRY HEAVEN'S HEARTBEAT

CARRY THEM SAFELY

HEALTHY BODIES CARRY HEAVEN'S HEARTBEAT!

TO CARRY — TO CONVEY FROM ONE PLACE TO ANOTHER,
TO BRING, TO TRANSFER, PENETRATE AND CAPTURE

If the Body of Christ worldwide is effectively going to reach this planet, then we seriously need to get *unified on the issues that matter.* As far as 'the world' is concerned, they observe the church quite sceptically. Our challenge is to not become so narrow that we judge them unfairly for this. Let's never forget that 'they' (those outside of Christ) are more than likely outside of Christ because the Light has not yet penetrated their darkness. Their understanding has not been enlightened and the love of God has not yet left its mark.

If we place ourselves where they are, what really matters? When Jesus was teaching His disciples the simplicity of reaching humanity, in essence He was saying, "above and beyond anything else, they'll know you are sent from My Father if you have love one for another AND FOR THEM"(John 13:34,35). So simple and yet so profound.

Honestly, does the world really care about our doctrine? Do they really give a second thought to our theology? Sorry to burst anyone's bubble, but no! The average person out there doing 21st Century life is not mesmerised by either of these. Nor are they interested in our eloquence and presentation, or our programs and events.

Society today is conditioned to a world full of talented, articulate, eloquent and personality-plus endowed people. If you don't understand what I mean, consider for a moment how spectacular and exciting the media and entertainment world is today.

PRACTICAL JESUS-CHRISTIANITY

So what is it that will move their hearts and arrest their attention? I believe *they want to see, and need to see, a sense of honesty combined with genuine expressions of love.* Love that is not merely in word alone but in deed also, love that is embracing and not judgemental, love that draws us beyond our personal comfort zone and into the very real world of hurting people. **Practical love that effectively leads people home to the author of love – God Himself.**

God's Kingdom is rapidly advancing across the earth, and there are wonderful men and women of God who labour tirelessly to this end. Only Heaven truly knows and chronicles the individual endeavours that go on behind the scenes, and one day all of eternity will resound with applause and praise. However, I am confident that none of us have witnessed the extent of our collective potential when it comes to effectively reaching hurting humanity. Our individual efforts are wonderful, but when we collectively bring our gifts, talents and resource together, our efforts move beyond the norm and into the "exceeding, abundant and above" (Ephesians 3:20). As each of our individual churches engages and harnesses collective potential, then choose to grow in Godly stature, the sky is the limit as to what we can accomplish.

In our church over recent years, we have been labouring to build wonderful facilities that will be a blessing to our community. Our church is not made up of rich people, but rather many generous and selfless people. If you measure what needs to be achieved financially, our individual contributions pale into insignificance, yet *together as a Body connected and contributing at every level,* we have witnessed a fabulous multi-million dollar facility emerge. Individually, could any of us achieve this? No way. Yet together, we are providing a brilliant facility which will enable the heartbeat of Heaven to come to the city of Sydney, and which will give future generations a great foundation upon which to build.

"When I look at My beautiful people, I call them a Body ... and it's about effective function." Heaven needs a vehicle.

When a person physically walks into a room, their "flesh and blood body" is the carrier that presents their true person. The "heart, soul, spirit and personality" of that person goes on display to anyone daring to observe. In like simple manner, the company of people defined as the Church of Jesus Christ is the vehicle who walk Christ into the room, or onto that delightful stage called Life.

HARMONY

Right now Heaven moves and responds to the heartbeat of our magnificent King. It is a phenomenon that God desires to be known on planet earth – 'Thy will be done on earth as it is in Heaven.' When strangers enter through the doors of our churches, what do they hear? Do they encounter a people marching or moving to the sound of a different beat (God's heartbeat) or do they encounter the strained sound of a people disconnected and non-functioning? Every time we *fail to understand*, every time we *fail to contribute*, every time we *fail to be knit together* (as we are commanded in Ephesians 4), we either intentionally or naively lessen the harmonious sound that calls God's sons and daughters out of their pain and into the arms of God.

The analogy of the human body is so amazing that it almost becomes breathtaking in its revelation. As I am neither scientist nor biologist, I am not going to attempt to exhuast the analogy of the body, because if I did this book would be 5,000 pages long. However, I have one thought – at the moment of human conception, the perfectly created person who has been in the heart and mind of God since before time, is miraculously nestled into the warm embrace of a place close to the natural mother's heart. The rhythmic beat of her heart is both reassuring and life to the unborn child. When that child exits the womb and enters life, I honestly believe that Heaven strategically goes to work to bring that child near to the Father's heart.

I pray that all of our churches will partner with Heaven and be mindful of this truth each and every time we gather together.

The fruit or *evidence* of God's Spirit is love, joy, peace, longsuffering, gentleness, goodness, meekness, self-control and faith (Galatians 5:22,23). Listen (and look) for these qualities next time you gather. Our *Heaven observed unity* is essential if we desire to see blessing in the House and across the earth.

'Behold, how good and how
pleasant it is for brethren to
dwell together in unity!

It is like the precious ointment
poured on the head, that ran
down on the beard, even the
beard of Aaron [the first high
priest], that came down upon
the collar and skirts of his
garments [consecrating the
whole body].

It is like the dew of [lofty]
Mount Hermon and the dew
that comes on the hills of
Zion; *for there the Lord has
commanded the blessing, even
life forevermore* [upon the
high and the lowly].'

[PSALM 133 AMP]

CHAPTER TWELVE

HEALTHY BODIES ARE BODY-BEAUTIFUL!

MASTERPIECES

HEALTHY BODIES ARE
BODY-BEAUTIFUL

BEAUTIFUL — TO DELIGHT THE AESTHETIC,
INTELLECTUAL AND MORAL SENSES

A s I began this chapter, I found myself lying on a beautiful beach on Australia's northern coastline. We were enjoying our annual Christmas vacation and the conviction to finish this book compelled me to start writing again. The sand up there is white, the sky blue, the water crystal clear and turquoise, and at twilight (if you're observant) the dolphins even come out to play. This north-eastern state in Australia has a catchy promotional slogan that says, 'beautiful one day, perfect the next!' Well, those two weeks proved to be exactly that.

As I lay scribbling on the sand, I found myself surrounded by countless suntanned, oil-clad bodies which encouragingly enough, came in every size, shape and age. One thing Brian and I love about this beautiful holiday location is how the sun and surf inspires you to live healthily. Despite the occasional ice-cream cone (or two or three), it motivates you to think healthy, eat healthy, exercise and be kind to your body. The end result is that we always leave feeling rested, inspired and more energetic than when we arrived.

Now I realise that this is the nature of a good holiday, but there's a powerful key here to maximising our health. I once heard someone say, "**If you sow energy and health, you'll reap energy and health.**"

In a spiritual sense, we have a heavenly responsibility to sow spiritual health and energy in order to reap healthy, energetic and achieving churches. Here are some 'Body-beautiful tips' that might help all of us do better at our 'Heaven-on-earth' mandate.

EAT GOOD FOOD

I think 'balanced' is the key word here. We need a *healthy balance* and approach to both life, our Christianity and the Word of God. Our church in Sydney is not perfect, but we *labour* to present a balanced Word that brings blessing and success to 21st Century life. We need to teach and relate God's ways to everyday people, doing everyday life, in everyday language. People want to know how to negotiate marriage and be around to celebrate the Golden Wedding anniversaries. They want to know how to raise beautiful children and present them to the world as beautiful adults. They want to know how to manage life and business affairs according to the precepts of our God who said, "I came to bring life and life more abundant" (John 10:10) and, "I desire that you prosper and be in health even as your soul prospers" (3 John 2).

Healthy functioning bodies labour to this end. We've all seen certain pockets of the Church go overboard on extremes of teaching. To be brutally honest, all it does is alienate 'normal' people from the Kingdom. If you are a leader we challenge you to be a wise steward over what you *feed your congregation*. A good shepherd ensures that his people are well fed and well nourished in the things that matter. And if you feel lacking in that area yourself, don't be afraid (or too proud) to venture beyond your own four walls to expose yourself to some of today's movers and shakers. God only knows too well, that none of us in leadership can do it all in our own strength. We definitely need to learn and glean from one another.

DRINK PLENTY AND DETOX REGULARLY

If you've ever read a health book or magazine, they'll tell you how essential it is to drink plenty of fresh, clean water. It helps to flush the system and keep everything moving (if you catch my drift). Now you don't need to be Einstein to apply this one spiritually. Every part of the body and every part of the local church (your local church) needs to benefit from the effect of plenty of water. Did you know that our own natural bodies are actually made up of 70% water? **God's Word is spiritual H^2O** and it will supernaturally keep us all clean, pure and uncontaminated by the rubbish and toxins that life can deliver.

The analogy could be applied in a thousand different ways, but here is an example. Anger and bitterness - there is not a human being on the planet who cannot get hot under the collar, yet what does the awesome water of God's Word say on this? "Be angry…but do not sin" (Ephesians 4:26). Hey, words of wisdom designed to keep us all 'body-beautiful' when it comes to *behaviour.* The Bible tells us that anger and bitterness can cause dryness of the bones. Dry, brittle bones can seriously impair a person's (or spiritually speaking, a church's) effectiveness.

EXERCISE REGULARLY

Oh dear … do we have to do this one! On our vacation Brian and I will walk (he runs actually) around seven to ten kilometres each day. We're both in our mid-forties and we have decided that exercise needs to become a lifestyle habit if we are going to cross the finish line strong for God. As Brian has often said, why assist the negatives of natural aging?

Our Christian experience is designed to be exactly that – *an experience.* There is nothing in the Great Commission that is a suggestion for any of us to sit on our rear ends and passively watch the world pass by. We are supposed to be running the race of life – active, agile, fit, willing and able. The Great Commission was GO!

Couch-potato Christianity is extremely unattractive and even offensive. The collective Body of Christ in each of our respective communities should be a company of active, healthy, involved-in-life, willing and available people, open to whatever initiative the Spirit of God prompts and/or stretches us towards.

As I mentioned earlier, our churches should examplify splendid, impressive, imposing and excellent specimens of the human race. We should be both naturally and spiritually healthy, strong and fit to the best of our ability. This has nothing to do with vanity or impressing others for the wrong reasons. It simply has to do with **WEARING OUR GOD WELL.** In his letter to Timothy, the apostle Paul exhorts us to be an *example in behaviour,* and John exhorts us to be an *example in health and blessing* (3 John 2).

(And forgive me if I'm taking this too far, but as we bask in His presence, our countenance shall also be 'Son-kissed!' Hey, the girls will love that one! Blame that romantic thought on that tropical Aussie beach.☺)

BATHE OFTEN

I wonder if we'll need soap in Heaven? Maybe not, because I somehow can't imagine Heaven making us all hot, tired and sweaty.

While we grace this planet, God has **called each of us to enter into His labour**. Even prior to the Fall Adam had a job to do – tend the garden. Now he probably got hot in the process because the Word says that God would come and fellowship with him in the 'cool' of the day.

Our spiritual labours will create the need for regular spiritual bathing. We have a great team of dedicated people working alongside us in the Cause, however the reality of working with others in an attempt to do the will of God causes all sorts of 'uglies' to rise to the surface. No point getting disillusioned. It's simply a fact of life and we all need to value the Father's invitation to regularly come before Jesus and let His forgiveness and cleansing wash over us.

Our *effectiveness, influence* and *appeal* will only be enhanced. Who wants to hang around the stench and staleness of undealt-with issues (use your imagination on that one)?

LAUGH LOTS

Nothing quite like a good belly-ache laugh to keep life in perspective. Even better if you are free enough to laugh at yourself. It may come as a surprise to some, but it's actually okay to enjoy life and feel good about yourself (and others for that matter). In fact, I'm sure that's how it is in Heaven and let's not forget that this entire book is dedicated to the thought of bringing Heaven into the House. Let's never forget that Jesus frequently nailed the Pharisees for their 'religious stiffness.'

It is also a fact that laughing releases the chemical 'endorphin' into our body, which *enhances health* and *adds to our sense of wellbeing*. I've also heard that *sex and chocolates* have the same effect (release endorphins that is). My advice - if sex is not on the agenda and chocolates aren't on the diet, then why don't you create the environment (or find an environment) where laughter is second nature. I pray that our churches will always be wonderfully magnetic places where the sound of laughter and good times is as natural as breathing.

DON'T FORGET THE BLOOD

Keep the blood flowing through your veins because life (both naturally and spiritually) is in the Blood. May we never, in our modern day presentation of the Gospel, forget how powerful and essential the precious blood of Jesus is.

The Word says, "They overcame by the blood of the Lamb and the word of their testimony and they loved not their lives even when faced with death" (Revelation 12:11). Constantly apply the *life and success building* principles, but

LAUGHTER IN THE HOUSE

also develop a personal revelation of the blood. The Passover still applies and over every single 21st Century believer, we find the precious blood of Jesus smeared. It may not be visible to the naked eye, but judgement recognises it and death has no authority over it. (Thank you, Jesus!)

HEAVEN'S PHYSICIAN

You and I live in a remarkable day and age. On the global scene, we are surrounded with and have easy access to phenomenal resource about our Christian walk, church growth and related issues. Flick through any of the leading Christian magazines or utilise the internet and you can access a leadership conference on practically any week of the year. There is no lack of wisdom, advice or motivational material to choose from. I don't have a problem with this. The only negative I can think of is that some Christians can become very *expert in theory*, but the planet is none-the-better because they never actually put their hand to the plough.

However, the point I want to highlight is – capitalise on the resource or advice available, but never at the expense of personal interaction with your Lord and God. May none of us (especially leaders) be guilty of going here, there and everywhere BEFORE WE LOOK UPWARD. I desperately want to grow in my ability to chat with God *first,* to ask His opinion *first,* to seek His approval *first* or when the challenge is on, seek His counsel *first*.

We are collectively called to be a Body effective on the earth. We have a very present and willing Heavenly Physician capable of healing, strengthening, empowering, enabling and directing us. Let us not be guilty of not availing ourselves of this most precious and wonderful gift.

REGULAR CHECKUPS

Here's a thought: hang out with other healthy bodies. They provide an interesting and sometimes enlightening *reality-check*, and again, when facing challenges, they will provide better perspective and wisdom than some perhaps less functional situations. The Bible says that 'iron sharpens iron' (Proverbs 27:17).

Don't be afraid to 'admire' other healthy bodies. The Kingdom is *NOT a competition* so we should be able to appreciate and compliment other wonderful churches who are prospering beautifully. Sadly, the overall landscape of the Church has not always been great at this. I am sure that petty jealousy, insecurity, territorial nonsense and even 'sibling rivalry' has been very disappointing to our loving Father in Heaven.

REPRODUCE AFTER YOUR KIND

So what 'kind' are you? What kind of people are emerging out of your church? (These are sobering questions, I know!)

I look at our three awesome kids. My sons have grown into strong, strapping, gorgeous young men (okay, I am their mother and I'm terribly biased) and our daughter is honestly delightful. By the grace of God, they all love God and are focused on the things that matter at their age. Brian and I have by no means been perfect parents and we admit to making mistakes, but I hope that the 'good in us' has rubbed off. I hope our children are a product of 'our kind.'

None of us are perfect yet. We'll save that assessment for the Father to make on Judgement Day, but I do hope our individual and collective desires *extend generously to the future generations.* Brian and I are very conscious that the choices that affect our health or ill-health when it comes to the Kingdom of God, will greatly affect our offspring (both natural and spiritual).

I often find myself speaking at women's conferences and I usually manage to challenge the women that, regardless of their age or whether they have natural children or not, we are all MOTHERS IN THE HOUSE. Being a mother in the House is actually an issue of maturity – and the nature of maturity is always to reproduce. May we all reproduce sons and daughters in the House, who have been nurtured in such a way as to bring glory and honour to God. Nothing more and nothing less.

Over the years on Mothers Day, our church has always tried to spoil the mums by giving them gifts such as a rose stem or a chocolate. Yet in recent years, I have tried to bring home the reality of this powerful principle by putting a gift into the hand of every female, regardless of whether or not she is a natural mum. I want *every woman* in our church (regardless of their age) to understand that they have the potential to be amazing WOMEN OF GOD and MOTHERS IN THE HOUSE who bring life and wisdom to everyone they meet.

AND FINALLY ... DON'T GET OLD BEFORE YOUR TIME

There is nothing sadder than seeing someone's physical potential cut short, because their natural body has aged or deteriorated before its time. Nothing as sad as encountering a church whose influence has failed to mature, and who has instead fallen victim to decline and stagnation. Age should not be our enemy. Longevity for a church body should not be a negative. Instead age should carry with it wisdom and experience and hopefully a story of distance travelled.

The Hillsong Church was once a young pioneer work. She continues to be a work in progress and has developed by the Grace of God into a place of maturity and influence. With any 'coming of age' there are always challenges to negotiate and new frontiers to scale. We realise that *impact and influence* can be seasonal, but Brian takes the attitude, "Why can't that season be a long season? Why can't we, with wisdom and stewardship, negotiate the seasons and stretch the influence?" Isaiah 54 is foundational to our church here in Sydney and says, "Enlarge, stretch, lengthen, spare not and strengthen." The promise of that chapter is one of expansion and influence that reaches beyond the present and well into the future. The fruit of that promise is that desolate hearts and desolate cities will once again be inhabited.

Our prayer for our church is that this vibrant, robust company of awesome people will continue to evolve into a House who, for the entire length of their days, will honour their King and bring hope to a needful planet.

"I call my beautiful people a House ... and it is about reaching the world."

ESSENTIAL
BODY-BEAUTIFUL TIPS!

(SPIRITUAL & NATURAL)

- DON'T TAKE YOUR BODY FOR GRANTED — IT IS YOUR *ONLY* CARRIER

- DON'T ABUSE YOUR BODY - WITHOUT IT YOU ARE *DEAD*!

- APPRECIATE ALWAYS

- NOURISH ALWAYS

- PROTECT ALWAYS

- PRIORITISE ALWAYS

- VALUE HEALTH AND WELLBEING

- SOW ENERGY IN ORDER TO REAP ENERGY

- ENLARGE, STRETCH, LENGTHEN, SPARE NOT AND STRENGTHEN THOSE (SPIRITUAL) MUSCLES

- MAKE TIME TO EAT, SLEEP, WORK, REST AND PLAY

PART THREE

'I CALL YOU A
HOUSE!'

HOUSE — A BUILDING
FOR HUMAN HABITATION, A
BUILDING FOR SPECIAL PURPOSE, A FAMILY,
A ROYAL DYNASTY, A PLACE
OF PUBLIC REFRESHMENT

"Then Jacob woke up and said,
'Surely the Lord is in this place,
and I wasn't even aware of it.'
He was afraid and said, 'What
an awesome place this is! It is
none other than the house of God
– the gateway to heaven!' The
next morning he got up very
early. He took the stone he had
used as a pillow and set it
upright as a memorial pillar. Then
he poured olive oil over it. He
**named the place Bethel –
'house of God'** – though the
name of the nearby village was
Luz. Then Jacob made this vow: 'If
God will be with me and protect
me on this journey and give me
food and clothing and if He will
bring me back safely to my
father, then I will make the Lord
my God. This memorial pillar will
become a place for worshipping
God and I will give God a tenth
of everything He gives me.'"

[GENESIS 28:16-22
(NEW LIVING TRANSLATION)]

CHAPTER THIRTEEN

HEALTHY HOUSES ARE AN ENCOUNTER WITH HEAVEN'S GATEWAY

WHAT AN AWESOME PLACE THIS IS! IT IS
NONE OTHER THAN THE
HOUSE OF GOD
– THE GATEWAY TO HEAVEN!

HEALTHY HOUSES ARE AN ENCOUNTER WITH HEAVEN'S GATEWAY

Bible legend Jacob found himself in an alien environment, far removed from the comfort and security of home. Tired and weary he laid down in the dust, rested his head against a hard stone and proceeded to dream a dream. He saw a ladder reaching from Heaven to earth, with the angels of God ascending and descending. God Himself spoke with him, confirming promises that belonged to both his ancestors before him and the generations who would follow him. When he awoke he exclaimed, *"God is awesome in this place. He was here all the time and I never even knew it! This place is none other than the House of God – the gateway to Heaven."* He then proceeded to make a memorial. He took the stone he had slept on, made it a pillar and declared that this revelation would become a place where people *worship God* and bring *a tenth of their income* as an offering to God.

MY ENCOUNTER

"This is none other than the House of God – the gateway to Heaven. God was here all the time and I NEVER EVEN KNEW IT!" I'm not quite sure how old Jacob was when this revelation hit him, but I walked this earth for 15 years, three months and 21 days before I encountered this truth. I was in biology class at school when a girlfriend witnessed to me and then invited me to her church that weekend.

My response was, "Oh Lilly, I believe in God, but I just don't think you need to go to church." Her gentle response was, "Okay, but do you want to come anyway?"

That Sunday evening, 7ᵗʰ May 1972, I walked into the Auckland Town Hall (New Zealand) where they held their Sunday church services. The Town Hall building was a structure I had been familiar with all my life, but that night it was different - very different in fact. I walked through the double doors and encountered an atmosphere that, on reflection, actually took my breath away. My little 15-year-old mind couldn't articulate what was happening, but I had entered 'another world' – the atmosphere, the environment, the presence was unfamiliar yet magnetic in its pull.

I watched, I listened, I sang along with this company of people who really looked like they believed in 'something.' When the preacher came out, I remember thinking, "Where are his robes?" He spoke on stuff that in reality went over my head, and then he made an appeal. He offered the people present an opportunity to know God and make Jesus Christ their Saviour. Between that moment and what I am about to tell you, I can't remember detail, except that tears welled up from the depth of my heart and I sensed a God I really didn't know, standing there saying "Come." I also sensed a battle happening, a battle between a negative voice in my head that said, "This is rubbish, don't listen" and a positive voice that said, "This is right." I clearly remember thinking, "All my goodness, all my perfection (I was a relatively good kid) was as nothing compared to this unknown and yet overwhelming person who was drawing me to Himself."

Leaving a literal pool of tears on the floor, I found myself at the front of the stage. With a crowd of others who had responded, I prayed a prayer of repentance and acceptance, and literally found myself reconnected to a God who had watched my every move since the day I was born. I remember both laughing and crying as the New Believer counsellor talked with me about the decision I had just made. As I drove home with my friends, I can still savour the feeling of sitting in the lounge room of my home and feeling distinctly different and distinctly clean.

I'm sure many of you reading this could share a similar story, but for those of you who can't, what actually happened to me back there?

I found myself in a place where God pulled back the heavens and (figuratively speaking) revealed the ladder that connects Heaven and earth, and mankind with their Creator. Upon reflection, it was as though He waited for the perfect moment (15 years, three months and 21 days) until I was seated in that earthly Town Hall, then He flicked the switch and stood at the top of the ladder and said, "Bobbie, here I AM. I've been here all the time and you never even realised. I've watched you all your life and tonight I'm throwing you the rescue line. I'm offering you My Son. Jesus will bridge the gulf that separates us. Welcome home, daughter."

I had found myself drawn to and into the House of God. In the city of Auckland at that time there were many churches (or Houses) that God could have drawn me to, but He drew me to the Queen Street First Assembly of God: a rapidly growing church which, back in the early 70s, was seeing an incredible move of God with unprecedented growth for that nation of New Zealand. It was a House that had attracted the favour of God – it was blessed with great teachers of the Word, it was blessed with an incredible music ministry that actually had global impact, it was blessed with an influential missionary program, it was blessed with a thriving youth ministry, it was expanding and influential and was gaining recognition from the nation in which it was planted. It became my spiritual home for four years, and I will be eternally grateful to the people of that church for the foundation they laid in my life.

THE ENEMY HATES THE HOUSE OF GOD

Sadly however, the leadership failed to negotiate some challenges that spiritually speaking 'come with the territory' and long story short, the House came under attack, the Body fragmented and a large proportion of the Family became scattered. Just prior to these challenges, I had become engaged to Brian and had moved on to join him, but I am saddened that such a magnificent House lost focus, momentum and (I guess) their destiny-path together. That church still exists today and is pressing on under different leadership, but the original blueprint that God had for that church, city and nation was without doubt *interrupted*.

I share that story because it is an all too common scenario around the earth. God waits centuries to orchestrate specific people, into specific environments, so He can reveal the rescue plan to a specific people, city and nation, and then, too often, we (His already redeemed children) fail to either understand or negotiate the part we play in this partnership, thereby slowing down, or worse still, sabotaging the plan entirely.

If you are a leader in God's Kingdom, then I challenge you to join me in living our lives in such a manner that we are not guilty of this. Life is one big learning curve, and no mistake is beyond correction, but *time* is short, *precious people* are self-destructing at an increasingly rapid pace and we have *the Father's business* to be about. The last thing I want to be guilty of is 'prolonging the process.'

A HOUSE PREPARING

"I call you a House … and it is about reaching the World." Salvation's Plan is to find eternally lost people, and then rescue, redeem and restore them. To do that God needs the 'perfect' environment to bring them to, and then nestle them into, until such a time as He literally takes them home to Heaven. The House of God is that environment and it should be amazing from the moment it comes into a person's line of vision.

Continue with me and let's discover what 'they' should discover from the moment they dare enter our driveways.

Maturing believers and leaders: I trust you have noticed the tenor of this book has just changed. Our focus is now totally *outward*. The House is designed to be a haven of blessing to the world we live in. Remember what Paul wrote:

> "I write these things unto you so that you may know how to conduct yourself
> in the House of God, which is the church of the living God, *which is the*
> *very pillar and ground of truth."* (1 Timothy 3:15)

Even as Jacob took the stone and made a *pillar* of his revelation, this same revelation of the Church is the *pillar and foundation of truth in our society*. Jesus said, "I will build my church and the gates of hell shall not prevail against it" (Matthew 16:17). I hope excitement has gripped your heart, because as God's 'willing and available kids,' we are now rolling up our sleeves and preparing the House for an awesome invasion of souls. I am confident that if God can find a House in preparation, He will move Heaven and earth to PUT THE HARVEST WITHIN THEIR REACH!

'THE EARTH IS THE LORD'S,
AND ALL ITS FULLNESS,
THE WORLD AND THOSE WHO
DWELL THEREIN.

LIFT UP YOUR HEADS,
O YOU GATES!
AND BE LIFTED UP, YOU
EVERLASTING DOORS!
AND THE KING OF GLORY
SHALL COME IN.'

[PSALM 24:1,7]

[Christmas 2000]

MY GORGEOUS **BEN** ...
LOVES LIFE, LOVES GOD, LOVES HIS MUM AND DAD,
LOVES SURFING AND SNOWBOARDING AND
WAKEBOARDING ...
LOVES TO PUT THE
CHRISTMAS TREE UP FOR ME ALSO!

CHAPTER FOURTEEN

A HEALTHY HOUSE IS AN ENCOUNTER WITH A DIFFERENT CALIBRE PEOPLE

PRINCESS
PAISLEY POSING
[COLOUR 2000]

A HEALTHY HOUSE IS AN ENCOUNTER WITH A DIFFERENT CALIBRE PEOPLE

CALIBRE — STRENGTH OR QUALITY OF CHARACTER,
ABILITY AND IMPORTANCE

If this REALLY is the House of God and the Gateway to Heaven; and if this REALLY is a place where people can encounter God and then learn to worship and know Him; and if this REALLY is a place that has the capacity to resource the salvation of the earth, then my question is – *what calibre people* should 'outsiders' encounter when they step out of their world and into ours? Should there be something different about us? Should there be something that marks us and separates us from the average person doing life on the planet?

I believe that such people *deserve* to find a company of people who have set their sight and the treasure of their heart on the very same things as God Himself. At the beginning of 2001, my husband began our year by challenging our people to make His world theirs. A revelation hit our spirits that powerfully and simply declared, 'You are my world!' It came forth in our teaching, our worship, our songs and our hunger and thirst to please God. It was a declaration that said, "God, You are not merely *a part of our world*, You *are* our world. There is no other, and we choose to treasure the very same things that You treasure."

As Brian opened up new direction and passion for the year, we found ourselves captivated by what our awesome God treasures. He treasures His magnificent Son *Jesus Christ*, He treasures *hurting humanity* and He treasures *His Church*. And so on the wings of these my heart began to leap regarding His House.

Let me ask the question again: What calibre people should a person who does not yet know Christ encounter upon entering this gateway, this House of God?

I believe they should encounter a *tender-hearted people*, who have made Jesus Christ, the darling of Heaven, their first love. They should encounter a *brave-hearted people,* because they have made His affection (the Church) their affection and they will brave whatever to cause her to advance across the earth. And they should encounter a *servant-hearted people,* because in becoming their Father's children, they have taken on the nature of Christ and will do whatever and pay whatever to walk lost brothers and sisters back home to the Father. Let me break this down and make it *tangible* in our world.

A TENDER-HEARTED PEOPLE

Think about this for a moment – when men and women, youth and children come close to the heart of God, *surely something has to rub off?* I'm actually not judgemental by nature, but when 'believers behave badly' this one question pops into my head, "Where is Jesus in this equation?" I'm not talking about the learning curves of life where we all make mistakes and learn thereby, but rather the reality that if Jesus was invited to be close to the heart of the matter, surely everyone would be behaving a whole lot differently?

I honestly believe that when outsiders brave our walls and enter our churches, they should encounter a people so extraordinarily different that their very lives call people home to Jesus. They should encounter a people whose entire manner and approach to life shouts that there is a God in Heaven who is fiercely interested in humanity.

Tenderness is defined as that which is *loving, affectionate, sensitive and easily moved to compassion.* Tenderness is something that we could probably write an entire book on, but I'll simply extend to you this one powerful thought: A PASSIONATE, PASSIONATE, PASSIONATE LOVE AFFAIR WITH JESUS CHRIST will paint tenderness across your life. In the same manner, a church that is PASSIONATELY IN LOVE WITH HER SAVIOUR will not only paint tenderness across that company of believers, but it will cause a House to emerge in that very community as an oasis in a dry and thirsty place.

[Laura Brett — Christmas 2000]

'LET THE WORDS OF MY MOUTH & THE
MEDITATION OF MY HEART
BE ACCEPTABLE IN YOUR SIGHT, O LORD,
MY STRENGTH AND MY REDEEMER.'

[PSALM 19: 14]

History's pages are indelibly marked with tender-hearts who changed the course of humanity. Abraham was a man so tender that the Word of God describes him as "a friend of God." Such was his tender relationship that when it came to two indescribably wicked cities, he almost reasoned God out of their due judgement. In Genesis chapter 18, Abraham implored, "Father, If you can find fifty righteous will you spare the city?" God's response was yes. "If you can find thirty righteous, twenty righteous, even ten righteous?" God was willing but alas, not even ten right living people could be found, so in an act designed purely to protect the future, God's hand was forced. Imagine if you and I could walk the earth with that kind of relationship. Imagine if it could be said of our individual churches "that they also were such a friend of God that they were able to *change the course of humanity for good.*" Such is the nature and reward of God's tender-hearts.

Joseph was another tender-heart – his tenderness positioned him with great influence in the then known world of Egypt. David, the shepherd boy who became a King – his tender love affair with his Creator became so anointed and breathed upon by the Holy Spirit that his love letters and love songs still cause our hearts to well and mount up to God. Imagine if our tenderness could testify of *similar influence.*

Tenderness is not something that is learned out of a textbook. It finds a home in us as we draw near to God and as we allow His precious Holy Spirit to take residence in our lives. **The awesome and magnificent Holy Spirit is madly attracted to people who passionately love Jesus.** He finds such a people and such a House irresistible. He is attracted to people who live to love Jesus and lift Him high across the earth. The Holy Spirit, the great *tenderiser* of life, causes us to become these tender-hearted people. In John chapter14, Jesus speaks tenderly of the Spirit:

"If a person [really] loves Me, he will keep My Word [obey My teaching] and My Father will love him, and We will come to him and make Our home (abode, special dwelling place) with him. Anyone who does not [really] love Me does not observe and obey My Teaching. And the teaching which you hear and heed is not Mine, but [comes] from the Father Who sent Me. I have told you these things while I am still with you. But the Comforter (Counsellor, Helper, Intercessor, Advocate, Strengthener, Standby), the Holy Spirit, Whom the Father will send in My name [in My place, to represent Me and act on My behalf], He will teach you all things. And He will cause you to recall [will remind you of, bring to your remembrance] everything I have told you." (John 14:23-26)

By loving Jesus, we attract and pull the Holy Spirit into our world and then *by choice*, the many and varied works of the Holy Spirit are permitted to have *their way*. In turn, we become tender-hearted, Christ-like people who are like a breath of fragrant air to a world hungry and suffocating for the tangible and tender touch of God.

A BRAVE-HEARTED PEOPLE

Did you ever see the movie *Braveheart*? Who could forget the piercing cry of William Wallis (played by Mel Gibson) as he was dismembered and executed for the cause of FREEEEDOOOMMM!

So what exactly is freedom? Freedom is defined as the state of living free, but perhaps we can describe it as a *king-dom* where absolute *free-dom* exists. This is exactly what God wants for us and this is exactly why Jesus paid the ultimate price. He purchased our freedom and a life beyond our wildest imagination – and the least we can do as *co-labourers* in this Cause is to allow our hearts *to risk being challenged.*

Bravery is defined as *the ability or readiness to face danger or pain.* Across the earth right now, there are Christians being persecuted and killed because of their faith. I stand in awe of their tenacity and courage, but the challenge on this page is to Christians who have made Christ their Saviour, yet are unable to step out of their 21st Century comfort zone or fear zone and make any worthwhile stand, sacrifice or contribution towards the extension of their Saviour's Kingdom. I'm talking about Christians who can't or won't step over the line. They verbally cry out for revival, but can't fathom, negotiate or manage church more than once a week. They verbally ask God to move on behalf of hurting humanity, but won't let God penetrate their finances. The gospel might be free, but trust me it costs a fortune to *effectively* spread it throughout the earth. They fantasize about the harvest coming to their church, but reality rudely bites when the harvest turns up on their doorstep unredeemed, unattractive and messy in the process.

You and I have found ourselves living in one of the most amazing times in history. As far as church history goes, we are possibly entering the most exciting times ever. As humanity's games become more lethal, our Father in Heaven desperately needs a company of people who are prepared to do whatever, and pay whatever to see truth (and therefore freedom) advance across the earth.

The answer to the world is JESUS. When I got saved as a teenager, I had Jesus-stickers all over my school bag and books. They read, "JESUS IS THE ANSWER." Yes, He IS the answer people are yearning for and **it is going to take a brave-hearted people to advance that Answer across the continents of this earth.**

I pray that whatever your calling or destiny-path, you will have the courage to face and do whatever it takes to advance His Cause. I am learning day by day that **leadership is about negotiating the frontline** for and on behalf of those present *and* those following. As far as the planet goes, our adversary, the devil, thinks the planet belongs to him. Our job is to advise him that he is sadly mistaken. Our job is to deny him his pleasure. In case you don't understand, Satan's pleasure is to make tangible his hatred of you. To deny him that pleasure requires a brave-hearted people. His objective is to obstruct the living and active Church of Jesus Christ so that Truth is quenched. Our job is to annihilate his obstacles and make a way for Truth to powerfully advance. Let's never forget or weaken our dear big brother John the Baptist's cry "PREPARE A WAY FOR THE LORD!" God is desperately searching the earth for a people who are *prepared to stand up and make a way for their King to advance.* (This is why the first song on the attached CD exhorts us to make a way for our glorious King.)

Consider what brave-heartedness and spiritual warfare might look like. Some people like to glamourise spiritual warfare and take it to strange extremes, but I honestly believe spiritual warfare is more about taking spiritual responsibility, stewardship and authority over what God has strategically *placed in your hand.*

So what has God placed in your hand? For pastors and leaders, it may mean being *prepared to pay the price that comes with the territory of leadership.* It may mean **refusing to abdicate when everything inside of you wants to lie down or lay down the sword.**

For every believer, spiritual warfare entails **aligning yourself with the Word of God and making a stand.** This may be manifest in refusing to ignore His principles regarding finances. Did you know that if every professing Christian on the planet chose to tithe (let alone give offerings), there would be enough finance to rescue this planet from its pain and misery? It may manifest in you **denying apathy its pleasure by becoming a radical, die-for-the-cause, passionate follower of Christ.** If rescuing some of our Father's children means that we host a gazillion-billion church services a weekend, then host a gazillion-billion services a weekend we will do.

We have one life, one moment to serve and an eternity to marvel at the opportunity we were given. I will never forget the powerful words of the Roman General Maximus in the film *Gladiator.* As he led his men into battle he declared, *"What we do in life echoes for all of eternity."* That one line, which almost caused my heart to jump out of my chest, may be the genius of a Hollywood scriptwriter, but it is still truth nonetheless. Our degree of brave-heartedness (or lack of it) will echo for all of eternity. I don't know about you, but I want history's pages and Heaven's chronicles to say of me and my church that they were a brave-hearted people, prepared to do whatever to advance their King's affection (the Church) across the earth.

When it comes to everyday Christianity, spiritual warfare for example, involves you maintaining the health of your cell group; the areas of church life that you are involved in; the weekend services that you attend; and the vision mandate over your church. It is about making sure that *whatever God has placed in our hands reaches its full potential!*

A SERVANT-HEARTED PEOPLE

When 'the world' steps into the House of God, another quality they should encounter is a breath-taking **company of servant-hearted people**; servant-hearted because they are their Father's children and are literally prepared to do whatever to facilitate His will on the earth.

When people visit our church in Sydney, a number of things impact them. For some, it is definitely the worship that captures their soul. For others, the breadth of leadership engages their attention. Others are captivated by the 21st Century Jesus revolution happening among the youth. However there is something *even deeper* that actually encompasses all of the above and is being used by God as a benchmark for others – it is the **spirit of servanthood.**

Now I've already said that Hillsong Church is by no means perfect, but I will say that God has done an amazing work in our people. In fact, the dedication and commitment that writes itself across the breadth of our church never ceases to amaze Brian and me. We are privileged to travel the earth and visit many wonderful churches, but we have *never quite* encountered such a generous, faithful, loyal and dedicated people.

Generally speaking this *generosity, faithfulness, loyalty, dedication and devotion* extends from the car park attendants, to the nursery workers, to the administration staff, right through to those who grace the platform. It is something that visitors constantly remark upon and constantly enquire as to how we make this happen. To be honest it is something that comes with the revelation of Family, Body and House. We are a company of people who are *discovering* what it is to be **Family-connected, Body-connected and House-connected.** We love the same things, we live for the same things and we are prepared to do whatever it takes to achieve His will. I know this all sounds terribly romantic and idealistic, but it is actually that simple. Brian and I love God and want nothing less than to please Him, be a blessing to His children and play a part in building their lives. Somehow in that simple equation, the people who have gathered alongside have caught the same heartbeat and have in turn become rather *contagious* in the process. I guess because we would do nothing intentional to hurt them and because we want only the finest in life for them, **they too are prepared to lay down their lives to also bring God's finest to others.** Combine this with the tangible favour of God (for which we are humbly mindful) and you have a powerful dynamic.

I'd love to tell you that what will make your church powerful and influential is a big, fluffy Glory-cloud from Heaven, but it's actually more about practical rubber-hitting-the-road Christianity. It is Christianity that is *comfortable in the limelight* (if that is the calling) but it is also Christianity that *is willing to sweep floors or clean toilets* (if that is what is most needful).

My husband says that you don't 'fluke' a great church in the same way that you don't fluke great kids or a great marriage. As I said earlier, many years of being knit together have produced a company of people who are prepared to do **whatever it takes**. It is for that reason that God has entrusted many talented and gifted *team players*, who at the end of the day could astound the world with their individual talent, but rather who **choose to position themselves as servants in the House.** It is a revelation that enables a person to realise that *their gift* is unto *the calling*, which is unto *the House*, which is unto *the Cause*. (By the way, God's glory in the coming days will attach itself to such spirited people and this we will witness more and more as we venture the Church into her future).

Our planet is splattered with many talented and gifted people who have no revelation that their gift has been granted for the local church where they are *supposed to be planted*. Many gifted Christians flutter around the greater Body of Christ and while their gift may bring enjoyment and a degree of impact, they will never know the **EXPANSE OF GOD'S GLORY** upon it because they see their gift as 'theirs to distribute as they see fit.' Of course we are all stewards over our lives, but let's never forget that "Every good and perfect gift comes down from above from the Father of Light" (James 1:7) and is given for a reason that is always bigger than ourselves. Such people often hold their gift tightly and while they might nominate who or where it will bless, they certainly have no revelation of it *unconditionally serving others*.

It is for this reason that our beloved friend and co-labourer, Darlene Zschech, is a mystery to many. Here is a beautiful woman of God, endowed with an abundance of gift and talent, yet many can't understand why she stays with "*that church in*

Australia." "Darlene," they say, "you can have the world. You are so gifted, so talented, why not break away and make it on your own?" But what they don't understand about this beautiful and Godly woman is that she has **a living, breathing revelation of the House.** She fully understands that *her measure* has been given by God to bless the House and that when the whole House grows in stature, it in turn has **the capacity to influence and possess the world** (in ways that exceed individual effort).

A few years ago, before Darlene had the global influence that she has today, she beckoned me to the edge of the platform after leading worship. With tears in her eyes she said, "Bobbie, it is such an honour, it is such an honour. I will do anything, I will sweep the floors, I will do anything, it is such an honour to serve my King with you." As it says in Psalm 84:10, "I would rather be a doorkeeper in the House of my God ..." than find fame and fortune outside the Kingdom. I think that moment may have been among a few other *defining moments* for Darlene that caused Heaven to say, "Mark that one for greatness. We can trust her."

Our planet is sadly littered with too many whose gift exceeded their character and ended up bringing their demise. To turn the glory upon oneself is actually incredibly dangerous. May we ever remind ourselves that in the Kingdom the 'spotlight' is not about fame or fortune, although these may become consequential, but it is simply about greater influence. The 'spotlight' simply allows a greater audience to see the glory of God upon a person's life. God said, "My glory I will not give to another' (Isaiah 42:8). His awesome glory is reserved for those who can humbly spread His fame abroad and not become seduced in the process.

This great calibre of spirit that I have been talking about is not uncommon in our church and I believe that it is this very *spirit of genuine servanthood* that is allowing our church to be contributing as it is to God's Kingdom today. I pray that we may always preserve and protect that spirit and that God will continue to smile upon it as we faithfully pass it onto the generations following. Without doubt, the generation emerging is the most gifted and talented to have ever graced this planet – *we have a large responsibility to help fashion them for greatness* (and greatness that will certainly exceed our own endeavours).

Turn the page and let's take a look at what 'calibre House' our beloved outsider should encounter when they decide to come visit our churches.

'I AM THE LORD;
THAT IS MY NAME, AND MY GLORY I
WILL NOT GIVE TO ANOTHER'

[ISAIAH 42:8]

HEALTHY HOUSES ARE AN ENCOUNTER WITH A DIFFERENT CALIBRE HOUSE

SMILING
CONFIDENTLY
AT THE FUTURE

HEALTHY HOUSES ARE AN ENCOUNTER WITH A DIFFERENT CALIBRE HOUSE

DIFFERENT — DISTINCT, SEPARATE, NOT THE SAME IN NATURE

S o precious reader, how are you going? More than likely I don't know who you are, but I want you to know that I love you and feel an incredible affinity towards you and your world. I believe in you, I believe in your potential and calling and I honestly desire only the best for you. Just felt like telling you that. Perhaps God prompted me to write this, because the truth is **He is 'mad about you' and wants nothing less than to see you excel in life.**☺

I think the foremost challenge we face as we take the Church into the 21st Century is the issue of *how* we 'do church' because, let's face it, God and His Word don't change. As some denominations struggle with declining attendance, there is an unprecedented parallel move of God sweeping the earth causing others to equally struggle as well but with the challenge of buildings that are too small to accommodate the throngs of people turning up.

I know that when the Spirit of God moves, people are drawn to Him as with a magnet. You don't need fancy buildings or fancy programs to witness an outpouring of God's Spirit, but long-term people need to be connected to and embraced into something substantial and lasting. My husband says that it is not hard to draw a crowd – bring in a renowned speaker, create an atmosphere and event, and bingo!

the crowd will come. However, to *build* an enduring work consisting of a company of dedicated and committed people is quite another matter.

WINESKIN ISSUES

What is the real issue at hand? The reality for many is that while their churches are relatively fine and good, there are countless pastors, leaders and believers who are frustrated to the back teeth because they are not seeing the growth, breakthrough or expansion they desire.

The Christian message is definitely not the problem. Not interfered with, its power and presence is ageless. Theologians do not need to tamper with, adjust, water-down or compromise the message of Jesus Christ *in an attempt to make church relevant,* because He is as relevant to today's generation as He has been to every other generation preceding ours.

Perhaps the 'wineskin' is the problem? The Word speaks of the insanity of trying to place new wine into old wineskins (Matthew 9:17). Church leaders around the earth (ourselves included) need to continually analyse the *relevance of how we communicate the message* of Jesus Christ. 'Wineskins' are the vehicles we use to present God's message. The problem with wineskins is that one generation can become rather comfortable with the wineskin that served their generation perfectly, but the same wineskin is totally unrelatable or inadequate for the emerging generation. While the message is good, the *application* of that message into people's everyday lives is lacking. "Why do we do what we do?" is a question we all need to continually ask ourselves. We ask this question frequently at Hillsong Church. Our focus, our message, and our mandate remains the same, but we frequently refine and redefine how we go about achieving the vision.

PARTNERING WITH HEAVEN

Assuming that the wineskins are good, why is it then that so many churches still struggle to achieve their potential? I address this carefully and humbly because we are not pretending to have this all worked out, but I think a major key **is creating and presenting an environment that God can actually work with**. Think about this for a moment – an environment that God can actually work with. We are exhorted in Revelation 22:17 to partner with Heaven – "The Spirit and the Bride (the Church) say come." In a way, we are called to actually make Heaven's endeavour easier. We are called to be co-labourers in the Cause.

Imagine an environment to which *the Spirit can easily draw a person.* Imagine an environment that *genuinely welcomes* the one whom God has been labouring for years to rescue. Imagine an environment that is, without reserve, *committed to helping a person in need*. If I was God looking out across a city and I could see such an environment, I would work overtime to position people there.

At one of our recent weekly Hillsong**women** meetings (which is our current vehicle for inputting into the lives of women), a woman responded to the salvation call and gave her life to Jesus. Afterwards I heard her story. Someone she knew had recently received Christ. This particular person came around to her house, bundled her into the car and without much explanation, had driven her to our church. He basically dumped her at our front steps and said, "Go inside, you need what's in there." She hesitantly walked up the steps and stood there, not really even knowing where or what she had come to. Thankfully our 'welcome team' were at their post. Thankfully they didn't ignore her. ***They noticed her***, welcomed her, embraced her and lavished her with the attention and affection she needed. To cut a long story short, that morning she encountered God in a life-changing way.

From Heaven's perspective what happened? I imagine God perhaps thought, "Okay, if I can manoeuvre events and can just get her on to those steps, I know those Hillsong**women** will take care of the rest." God is sovereign, and of course He can move Heaven and earth, but let's never forget that He works with humanity. Humanity has a will – they can be willing or unwilling. On that morning, we could have missed a precious opportunity if one of our ushers had been unwilling to be sensitive and available.

TRUSTWORTHY

Our challenge is to present the House in such a way that it is **irresistible to God** and **irresistible to mankind**. Irresistible to God, because He can look from Heaven and say, "I trust my kids in *that* House" and instruct His angels to cause His lost sons and daughters to collide with *that* company of people down there. "Just get them as close as you can," He will say, "because I know that they'll be on the lookout; they'll take them by the hand and walk them into My Presence." Irresistible to mankind because who can resist an outstretched hand and smiling face?

Allow me to walk you through the House of God and suggest a few tips on how *we together* can create an encounter too irresistible to refuse – an encounter where the **atmosphere** is warm, embracing and accepting. An atmosphere where the door is open, the lights are on and the welcome mat has been laid out. An atmosphere resounding with music, energy, life and laughter. An atmosphere dripping with excitement, noise and connection. An atmosphere tangible with people, children and family everywhere. An atmosphere that is clean and fresh with a sweet-smelling aroma. An atmosphere where friends, travellers and strangers are anticipated. An atmosphere that reminds you of home – safe, secure, divine. An atmosphere where the spiritual fridge is full and overflowing in preparation ... and where the men, women, youth and babies in the House are breathtakingly gorgeous.

Does this sound too good to be true? Well, then walk with me through these next few pages and let's see if this cannot become reality.

CHAPTER SIXTEEN

HEALTHY HOUSES HAVE A MAGNIFICENT WELCOME MAT!

My daughter Laura (left) – September 1999

FRIENDS FOREVER

[LAURA AND CHANTELLE –
ON THE EVE OF A NEW MILLENNIUM]

HEALTHY HOUSES HAVE A MAGNIFICENT WELCOME MAT!

WELCOME — A KIND AND GLAD RECEPTION

THE WELCOME MAT! At Hillsong Church we've always had one, but we've only recently referred to it as such. The Welcome Mat! What is it, why is it so important and where does it begin and end? By the way, I'm not talking about a literal mat at the door, although they have been known to reduce the wear and tear on the carpet and the vacuum cleaners!

The Welcome Mat begins with everyone learning what it is to become a 'bringer.' Bringers are people who will not merely *invite* friends, family, colleagues, neighbours or even strangers to their church, but they will actually **go out of their way to bring them**. This may sound elementary or obvious, but you might be amazed at how many Christians are either embarrassed or not confident to invite friends to their local church. (I am constantly surprised at how many visitors come to Hillsong Church who openly admit that they brought their friends here to get them saved because they didn't feel comfortable to take them to their own church. We love visitors, but you have to agree that something is wrong with this picture).

The analogy of the House hasn't weakened. Here's a question – how many of us are *proud enough* and *in love enough* with our church to invite people over? "Hey, come to my House, come to my church, you'll love it. Mum and Dad (spiritually speaking) will love you to bits – they'll make you feel at home, they'll feed you. There's heaps of cool people at my house; you'll love it. Come!"

Excuse me if I get a little in-your-face here, but evangelism (especially in western culture) almost rests on this simple and yet profound thought. *If we all took the responsibility of making the House magnificent*, people would be proud to bring their loved ones to it. They would feel confident that they would be welcomed, smiled upon and loved. They would be confident that nothing embarrassing and weird was going to happen (and I'm not talking about compromising the Presence or Word of God here). They'd be confident that there would be something nourishing on 'the table' that would feed their friend's hungry heart, and even if that invited person did not respond immediately to the love of God, they'd be confident that the environment was embracing and normal enough to draw them back again.

BEGINS WITH AN INVITATION

The Welcome Mat begins with the invitation. An invitation that simply says "Come and see! Come and see a Man who will love you to bits! Come and see all His other amazing kids. Come and see!" May I remind you of how all the disciples got to be together? One day one of them met Jesus and Jesus said, "Follow Me." Then one after the other, they grabbed their friends, family, whoever and said words to this effect, "COME AND SEE … come and see a Man who has … ." (For this reason, we constantly make 'invitation cards' available to our people, so that they have something tangible to put in a friend's hand when they make the invitation.)

REACHES INTO THE COMMUNITY

The Welcome Mat reaches into the community. In places where the Spirit of God is truly moving, gone is the narrow mindset that had the Church hiding from the big, bad world. Jesus said, "Go into all the world and make disciples of all men"(Mark 16:15). The tenor of His entire message was, "Go into all the world, make friends with them, *tangibly* show them My love and before you know it, you'll have their respect and they'll be hungering and asking questions about Our Father."

Every church needs to learn how to practically reach out into the community because we are called to be *bridge-building people.* That means we have to get over 'their sin' and love them for who they are – people who just don't know God yet. If they don't know God, why on earth would their *lifestyle* be squeaky clean?

Jesus did not have a problem mixing with the world. He hung around them, He embraced them, and He certainly didn't freak out when their sinful humanity surfaced. He salted their lives, He made them thirsty and when their thirst got the better of them and they had to ask, He had the answers for them. We are called to do likewise. Every week we see increasing numbers of people coming to Christ because our people are *real enough to be attractive to enquiring, thirsty people*. All they do is engage interest and then invite them to (a loving and exciting) church. Once inside the House, the *Spirit of God* and the *Word of God* goes to work and draws them to Jesus. How hard is that?

I was once speaking at a conference in Los Angeles. A gorgeous young man responded and gave his life to Jesus. As the meeting finished, he approached me and said, "I liked everything you said, but I'm gay and I don't think there's anything wrong with that!" As we sat on the step, I took a deep breath, smiled and thought to myself, "There is no way I am going to *legislate lifestyle* on this young man, who is *only minutes old in God.*" So I grabbed his hand and said, "Do you know what? You have just met God – how amazing is that! You have lived your life on an earthly level, way below what He intended. Right now, if you want it, a whole new world has opened up and you have a chance to open God's Word, talk to Him and discover for yourself *the son that you really are.*" Afterwards the new believer counsellor said to me, "What did you say to that guy? He's totally at peace and there is no sign of offence." What did I do? I simply loved a brand new brother and made room for *the Spirit of God (not me) to reveal truth regarding his sexuality.*

The Welcome Mat begins in the community. Right now visualise it stretching across your community.

RESEMBLES A RED CARPET

The Welcome Mat should resemble a red carpet! Now here's a thought! Why shouldn't the Welcome Mat be a Red Carpet? Why shouldn't we take the attitude that *every visitor and every person is a special guest,* worthy of Red Carpet treatment. We should do this, and it would bring honour to our King. As far as Heaven is concerned, every single human being is a V.I.P. – a Very Important Person. As Christians we often say, "You are so valuable. If you were the only person on the planet, Jesus would still have died for you," yet how often does our behaviour reflect the opposite?

BEGINS IN THE CARPARK

The Welcome Mat actually begins in the car park! Once an 'unchurched' visitor has gathered enough courage to venture onto our property or respond to an invitation, we need to be *on the alert for their approaching arrival.* Don't underestimate the tactics of the enemy. If he gets a sniff that someone is approaching 'the House of God – the Gateway to Heaven,' trust me, he'll work overtime to sabotage that encounter. So we need to work smarter. We need to cut him off at the pass and remove the possibility of someone thinking, "I'm lost, and I don't know where to go. This is too hard. I'll just drive out again and go home." We should almost anticipate this and make sure that the car park welcome is well covered.

At Hillsong Church we have learnt to station people all over the car park (or at least we try). We roster our young people out there and people constantly comment on the friendly, smiling, zany, slightly-off-the-planet, non-conventional young people who make approaching church a delightful experience. (I cannot drive past any of them without blowing them a kiss).

I thank God for a team around us who are constantly pushing out the boundaries when it comes to hospitality. If having umbrellas in bad weather to help people get inside is the second mile, then so be it. If having a strategy to help solo parents get into church with a handful of kids is the second mile, then so be it. **Second mile Christianity is very attractive to Heaven.**

The Welcome Mat should be well thought out and planned, and we should believe for it to have the breath of God upon it.

The *team of people who welcome and embrace people are integral in the scheme of things.* I could give you methods and ideas, but essentially you need to look at your community and ask yourself the questions: How can we effectively welcome these people? How can we make them feel like they are the most important people on the planet? How can we make them feel like we've been waiting a lifetime to meet them? How can we negate fear and remove all the obstacles? How can we effectively prepare the House for *invited visitors, strangers* and *returning prodigals*?

In reality, this **Welcome Mat is the doorstep that precedes Heaven.** When 'travellers in life' step over that threshold they are in essence entering a brand new world – a world that has the capacity to reveal Heaven itself. How exciting is that? It kind of puts a whole new perspective on the ushering team, doesn't it?

CHAPTER SEVENTEEN

HEALTHY HOUSES RESOUND
WITH HEAVEN

'THEY SHALL POUR FORTH LIKE A FOUNTAIN,
THE FAME OF YOUR
GREAT AND ABUNDANT GOODNESS'
[PSALM 145:7]

HEALTHY HOUSES RESOUND WITH HEAVEN

TO RESOUND — TO FILL, ECHO AND MAKE FAMOUS

Healthy Houses *resound with the literal sounds of Heaven.* I'm sure Heaven will exceed our wildest imagination, but this side of eternity we have a responsibility to do our best to do God proud! Psalm 34:8 says, "Oh taste and see that the Lord is good." God is good, Heaven is good, and Heaven-on-earth here and now should also be good. When strangers to the things of God cross that threshold they should encounter *an atmosphere that drips with Heaven.*

LIFE

They should encounter the sound of Life. Jesus said in John 10:10, "I am come that you might have life and life more abundant" – not death, not misery, not negativity, not hopelessness, but LIFE!

Where there is life there is hope. Ecclesiastes 9:4 says it like this, "He who is joined to all the living has hope." Paul also wrote about hope, saying that it is "the anchor to the soul" (Hebrews 6:19). When unbelievers enter our churches, this very *atmosphere of life has the spiritual capacity* to penetrate their hearts with hope – hope that there is a better world; hope that perhaps there are answers within these four walls to their questions and needs; hope that someone can give them tangible direction and hope that might bring clarity to the penetrating question within every human heart – "Please someone, give me a reason for my existence."

CONNECTION AND UNITY

They should encounter the sound of connection and unity. I've already laboured these thoughts in previous chapters, but close your eyes and picture this scene. I know it's hard to close your eyes and read at the same time (☺) but imagine someone has invited you to a party. As you approach the front door you can hear the buzz, you can hear the music, you can hear the sounds of uncomplicated people enjoying themselves. Excitement rises in your heart because something good is happening and you sense that you are about to *become a part of it.*

Well the party is called LIFE WITH GOD and the above should describe 'the approach' to every church.

I don't know what your local church looks like, but ours is exactly as I have described. Essentially our church is one big, happy, noisy party. We love God, we love life, we celebrate our *togetherness* and it is very attractive. It's the kind of atmosphere that causes people to line up for church, and then has them stay afterwards. You can always tell the health of a place by how many linger afterwards. I think this defines a healthy House – nobody wants to go home because it's been so good.

And it is noisy! Connection is noisy. Of course there are times when we 'hush' because Abba Father has made tangible His presence, but I've never known a house full of healthy kids to be overtly quiet. Traditional religion has painted a picture of the Church as, "Shhhhh, be quiet, don't speak, don't make any noise, don't be real, you might offend God." Well I've got a sneaky suspicion that Heaven is anything but quiet. Revelation tells us that there will be a moment when all of Heaven and earth is silenced as we honour and value the prayers of the saints, but honestly, I think Heaven *resounds with thunderous noise and celebration to our King.* I think God is very comfortable with the sounds of His children enjoying themselves.

On this note, you can also tell that 'the Family' have been in the House by the mess they leave behind. It's no use getting all hot and bothered about the mess that comes with the crowd. We have literally thousands pass through our House weekly and we can show you the mess to prove it, but no one is having a nervous breakdown over it (least of all the amazing team of ushers who clean up afterwards). We have truly awesome, mature 'Mums and Dads' (of all ages) in the House, who joyfully stay back to put the House back in order. Such is the nature of a healthy house.

THE SOUND OF HEAVEN

They should encounter music resounding from Heaven above. Cathy Lechner is a dear friend to our church, and the very first time she ventured onto Australian soil, she prophetically spoke over my life. Her prophetic gift is probably the strongest we have ever witnessed. She had no idea who I was, what we were about or the nature of our church. As she prophesied about the major areas of our ministry, her voice softened as she said "…My song, My song, My song is in your House … ." As Cathy ministered to me, I could almost hear the Father in her voice, saying "My song is in your House."

I know that God has graced our church with an opportunity that is truly a gift from above. So many of our songwriters have had words spoken over their lives that sounded like this - "I will send My angels to whisper in your ear, songs such as have never been heard in all the earth." It is for that reason that our hearts rise in love and appreciation to God for allowing us to have a part to play in bringing a sound from Heaven to earth. When people enter these doors – the literal House of God, the Gateway to Heaven – they should hear something that sounds different from what they know. It is more than lyrics and melodies, they are songs from Heaven that carry *the breath of God to dry and thirsty hearts.* I love our church because those gifted and anointed to lead in this arena have devoted themselves to 'their secret place with their King,' and they return to us with songs from another world. They bring a taste of Heaven to earth that refreshes and ignites the hearts of humanity. Their songs give us a beautiful vehicle upon which to express our love to God… and *the whole experience of unrestrained, extravagant worship is captivating beyond expression.* (Please God, may our love for you never waver or cease; and may the future be overwhelming as we draw closer and closer to your Presence.)

"I am the Lord; that is My name! And my glory I will not give to another, nor My praise to graven images. Behold the former things have come to pass, and **new things** I now declare; before they spring forth I tell you of them. *Sing to the Lord a new song,* and His praise from the end of the earth! You who go down to the sea, and all that is in it, the islands and coastal regions and the inhabitants of them [*sing a song such as has never been heard in the heathen world*]." (Isaiah 42:8-10 AMP)

(When I read that scripture, I affectionately imagine that the end of the earth and " the islands and coastal regions" are definitely talking about Australia!☺)

DANCING, REJOICING, GOOD TIMES

They should encounter the delightful sounds of dancing, rejoicing and good times. Such was King David's encounter with God that he danced – body, soul and spirit celebrating. I think there is actually nothing more irritating to the enemy than God's people dancing across life.

'Delirious' are a band of young Englishmen who have also inspired many with a refreshing new sound of praise and worship. One of their songs declares a people passionate for God, who *"dance upon injustice."* If you would like to seriously intimidate the enemy, then dance like an army upon injustice. Battles are won as we go into battle rejoicing, singing and dancing in our spirits. A movie was made called *Remember the Titans*. Based on a true story, it told of an American high school football team who fought for unity between black and white. In the face of racial prejudice, such was their hard-fought battle for unity that they would 'dance' out onto the field and take victory every time.

In my book *I'll Have What She's Having,* I wrote this in the epilogue: "What is happening in the church today is wonderful. Nowhere in the world do you have the generations coming together in such unity. *Nowhere but in the Church* do you have youth dancing and rejoicing and joining vision with an older generation. *Nowhere but in the Church* can complete strangers walk through doors for the first time and be genuinely welcomed as if they were long lost family. This is happening in the Church of Jesus Christ in the world today. It is happening across the nations. It transcends denomination and culture, and it is *the Spirit of the living God."*

Healthy houses resound with the high praises of God. It is magnetic to the host of Heaven and it is magnetic to humanity. When we worship God with total abandonment, we find ourselves in the company of angels, and that is when we can humbly and boldly boast that *Heaven is in the House.*

CHAPTER EIGHTEEN

HEALTHY HOUSES ARE BEAUTIFULLY APPOINTED

ART – HUMAN CREATIVE SKILL
"OH TO BE CREATIVE ARTISANS UNDER
HEAVENLY INSPIRATION!"

HEALTHY HOUSES ARE BEAUTIFULLY APPOINTED

APPOINTED — EQUIPPED, FURNISHED, A DIVINE PRESCRIPT

Now fellas, please don't switch off at this point☺. You are integral in this equation because as the MEN IN THE HOUSE you have the clout to make things happen. In fact we love it when you pave and make a way for the House to be magnificent. When I find myself teaching women, I simply encourage them *to be magnificent partners with the men that God has yoked them to* – be that either in marriage relationship or be that with the various men they find themselves doing life with. We need each other, and for the House of God to be beautiful we also need each other's strengths and gifting.

Healthy Houses are beautifully appointed. What do I mean by that? The House should be BEAUTIFUL. It should not be broken down, tatty, neglected, dated or dirty, but rather the best we can make it. Having a beautiful church facility is not solely reliant on finances, but it is more about *furbishing and furnishing the House with a sense of pride and excellence.*

Again, the analogy of 'Family, Body and House' applies here. **The House of God down here on earth should be STUNNING**. It should reflect well on our Creator and it *should impress the world.* Yes, I make no apology for this statement. For too long, an impoverished mentality in the Church has weakened the presentation of the world's greatest message. We don't want the world who God so dearly loves to look at the Church and think: "Well, if God is so amazing, how come those Christians are so drab and boring, and look as if they have come out the Ark?" or "If God is the Answer, how come so many of them live on the bread line and struggle to survive?" or "If God is so brilliant, how come that church on that street corner cannot mow the lawns or tend their gardens?" And worst of all, when passing by magnificent cathedrals that drip with opulence, "If God is so wonderful, how come nobody is there?"

BREATHTAKING AND GORGEOUS

I know this is a bit in-your-face, but someone has to say it. For too long, the enemy has kept huge pockets of the Church contained and impoverished through small-thinking. Sadly, this is not a true representation of our incredible King. This may come as a shock to some, but I don't think God has a problem with lush or lavish things. Now I'm certainly not suggesting you can make 'lush and lavish things' an idol in your life, but I'm talking about *the splendours of our King finding a home in our lives.*

God does not have a problem with 'beautiful things' because He Himself is an awesome Creator. Take a good, long look at creation. He has furbished the planet magnificently, and woven it together with great love, care and creative genius. With painstaking intricacy He has fashioned colour and texture together and IT IS GORGEOUS! It is breathtaking in its beauty and splendour, and it is reflective of our God in Heaven. He also gave it to us as a playground to enjoy!

Now stop and consider the House of God. Should not the House of God also reflect the same? Should not the place that God inhabits when we praise and worship Him be beautiful? Should not our presentation and appointment of the House be divine? Should not the House of God be tended and manicured and cared for? Should not our gardens and driveways be perfect? Should not the House be clean, fresh and inviting ... and lavished every now and then with a little T.L.C.(Tender Loving Care)?

Again, I am not saying this in the context of extravagance, but rather in the context of us loving the House in such a way that we take care of it. When people pioneer a new church, of course money and resource are a stretch. It is exactly the same when a young couple start out in life together. Unless they have been blessed by wise parents who may have given them a great start in life, most have to start somewhere and build upwards. When Brian and I bought our first home, it was about the size of a shoe box! Every room came off the dining area – the kitchen, laundry, bathroom, bedroom and lounge room. When we sat people down at the table, you couldn't move from one side of the house to the next. We were just starting out in ministry and we had no finance for anything except the mortgage. However this is the lovely nature of beginnings. Today, we have grown in life and stature, and because we have put God first in our lives (i.e. build God's House and He will build yours) and because we have grown in our revelation of Godly finance and blessing, we now live in a much larger house. Even though there are still things to do, we really lack for nothing.

It is the same in church life. Young pioneer churches have to begin somewhere, but after years of growing in wisdom, grace, understanding, prosperity and stature, they should see the House increase and blossom.

AN EXAMPLE OF EXCELLENCE

A healthy House should present well. Regardless of what stage your church might be up to, it should still be an *example of excellence in your community*. Most people respect 'small beginnings' and won't judge you, for example, for not having state-of-the-art furnishings, but at least keep what you do have clean and presentable. I'm labouring this point because I think it's important.

We need to train ourselves to 'love the House' in the same way that I hope we love our own homes. It is actually essential to have a spring clean every now and then, send broken and worn-out furniture to the garbage tip and encourage people to take pride in the House. Budget for repair and maintenance. For some these thoughts are second nature and obvious, but others need to be prompted to think like this. It's no different from a natural family. All families need to train children how to pull their weight and respect the home in which they live.

Our challenge at Hillsong Church is that young or new people coming in now can *easily take for granted* what has taken others years to achieve. A newcomer can easily forget or be ignorant of the sacrifice made by someone else which purchased the seat they're sitting on. No one wants to be a 'nag' but I can remember stopping by at youth one night to discover a bunch of big, gorgeous, burly boys having races with the brand new, roller chairs that we had just purchased for the parent's feeding room. Quietly I cornered a leader and with a smile on my face (and a look in my eye) said, "See those chairs – I waited a long time to buy them. They cost big bucks, so put them back and lose the race track!"

It is not often we have to say this, because we endeavour to train our staff and leaders (and hopefully our people) to 'take ownership and notice things.' For example – notice that the garbage bin is overflowing, notice that the toilet paper has run out, notice the stain on the carpet, notice that the colour scheme sadly clashes. Ownership means not only to notice but take responsibility and do something about it.

Hey, if visitors were coming to your house for a special party, there is no way you'd leave the garbage at the front door, would you? Yet it is amazing how many churches forget these little details. Old hawk-eye here notices everything... but do you know what is even more remarkable – my husband who carries an enormous amount of responsibility, will walk into church and notice the same? He'll even notice *dusty corners or fluff on the carpet.* (Mind you, he doesn't notice it at home. Actually he probably does, but I think it's called 'selective male blindness.') Praise God that we have key players on our team who take responsibility to remove these smaller details from our lives and release us to think about the 'big picture.'

EXCEEDING, ABUNDANT AND ABOVE

I think some 'contained' Christians are going to get to Heaven and get a bit of a rude shock. They are going to discover a place full of beautiful mansions, beautiful furnishings and Heavenly opulence, and they might find themselves thinking, "That's a bit over-the-top! That's a bit excessive!" But God IS excessive! He is generous and over-the-top. By His own admission He is an "exceeding, abundant and above all" God. He said, "Eye has not seen, ear has not heard, neither has it entered into the hearts of men, the things that I have prepared for them" (1 Cor 2:9). Now that doesn't give us licence to be idiots and take blessing, prosperity and style to obnoxious lengths. It does not give us licence to be *wasteful*, but it does give us *permission* to present the House beautifully and live our lives in such a manner that 'those outside the Kingdom' look on in envy. We should be enviable in the purest sense, because we are a people blessed and lavished upon by our Heavenly Father. According to the Amplified Bible 'blessed' is defined as "blessed, happy, fortunate and *to be envied.*"

May I encourage you to view the House from Heaven's perspective: Don't be afraid of style and excellence, and don't be contained by old religious mindsets that have you doing things in a certain way because "That's the way it's been done for centuries." Never forget to *serve the generation you live in.* Of course our individual style is determined by our own personality, so the way you will decorate and present your church will reflect 'you' which is actually great, but always be mindful of the broader spectrum of people you want to reach.

For example, as we all stretch and build bigger facilities, we can't be decorating those larger scale auditoriums in the same way we decorated our little living rooms. There is a difference between decorating on a large corporate scale and decorating on a smaller domestic scale. On that note, it might be good to learn the difference between personal taste, good taste and bad taste. Brother or Sister so-and-so might be dear, sweet people but maybe they're not the best or most gifted to be choosing the colour schemes. (But remember, the colour of the carpet is not worth having a church split over.)

And when it comes to special events ... don't be afraid to put in a little extra effort. For some people, being innovative and creative comes easier than it does for others, however this is where the big, broad, colourful family of God is amazing. As you draw people into the adventure of awesome church life, you gather not only their commitment and passion, but also their gifts and talents. I guarantee that there are 'surprise people' all over your church just waiting to be discovered.

Our God is a truly creative God. He created us in His image and I know that **within all of us are creative boundaries just waiting to be pushed.** We live in a secular world that is stretching those boundaries daily – let's not colour and limit their perception of God by not harnessing this same creativity ourselves.

CHAPTER NINETEEN

HEALTHY HOUSES
FEED THE HUNGRY

HEALTHY HOUSES
FEED THE HUNGRY

L et's imagine that by the grace of God, the invitations have gone out, the recipients have responded, they have found their way to the 'House' and they're not fearful to enter. We've welcomed them in the car park, on the front steps and at the door. They're somewhat overwhelmed because they aren't even inside the building and already they feel as if they've made fifty new friends! Their attention has been captured by the welcoming hands, the warm smiles and now … they are about to be tangibly drawn towards the Throne of God.

You may call me a romantic idealist but I don't see why it can't be like this. Why can't we present our King's House in such a way that lost hearts are immediately captivated?

Once people are inside and the service begins, our sole responsibility is two-fold. Firstly, it's to make sure that we *create an environment* that will *draw the presence of God,* and secondly, it is to *present the Word of God* as best we can. All our programming, advertising, event management and trimmings are merely tools whereby *we bring the people to the House **so that God can connect with them.***

As leaders, our prime responsibility is to create an environment that will attract

Heaven. In other words, our focus is set on loving, praising and worshipping Jesus. Our songs and hymns are for no other reason than to love and lavish God with the adoration that He is worthy of. In the process of magnifying Him, His Presence will draw near – the person of Jesus Christ and the Holy Spirit (if invited) invades our space, and when 'outsiders' encounter this, they are forever affected. As Marilyn Hickey says, "Exalt Jesus and God will turn up and show off." Some respond immediately to Him, others will process the experience, and some will say, "No thank you." While we cannot legislate a person's acceptance of God, what we can do is love, encourage and exhort them to respond to His love. Should they refuse, we are commanded not to cease loving them.

Our other responsibility, especially as leaders, is to present, bring and teach the Word of God as best we know how. As leaders, if we can remember these two simple things, it will remove much of the stress and strain of ministry. You and I in our mere humanity can accomplish little, but it is the *power of His presence* and the *power of His Word* that will arrest a person's heart and bring change. We are simply vehicles through which He can move. If you can capture the simplicity of what I am saying, I know it will bring release into your ministry.

GOD HONOURS PREPARATION

Our dependency on God does not mean that we *become lazy* and take a passive attitude that says, "It's all up to God!" Yes, it is all God, but we must be diligent. For example, our worship team must prepare and press for excellence. It is a huge responsibility to be granted the privilege of leading God's people into His presence, and it requires prayer, preparation and diligence. Practice makes perfect. Practice allows you to relax and then follow the ebb and flow of God's Spirit because you are not stressing out over unrehearsed notes, chords or words.

God not only honours but He actually loves preparation. It proves to Him (and others) that we are serious and are not taking the opportunity lightly. Pastors all around the earth will tell you that there is nothing more frustrating than having to work with a team of singers and musicians who have no understanding of this. If you are a pastor and you are facing a shortfall in this area of your ministry, then realise that ultimately you are responsible. Either correct the problem or pay the price to position your team around others who have a revelation of how essential all of this is.

Our stewardship over this aspect of ministry is crucial in effectively ushering in the Presence of God. Of course we can encounter God without a whizz-bang worship team, but when you *partner heartfelt, extravagant worship with the Spirit-breathed Word of God, you have a combination that arrests the human heart like none other.* Then of course, once the atmosphere has been created, once the presence of God is in the place, once hearts have softened and opened – then the Word comes out onto the table, Heaven invades our world and amazing things begin to happen.

SET THE TABLE BEAUTIFULLY

Our responsibility as leaders is *to prepare and set the table beautifully,* and then trust God to arrive with food perfect to every person's need. Of course, He doesn't literally arrive with the food – He feeds us through the faithful lips of His servants – the men and women He has entrusted to teach and preach. Out of their mouths, out of their preparation, out of their seeking, their thirsting and their journey walked with God, the 'Word in season' will fall on hungry hearts and will not return void. When my husband was about forty-five years of age someone asked him how long it took him to prepare a sermon. His reply was, "A few hours, ... and forty-five years."

> "So shall My word go forth from My mouth, it shall not return to Me void,
> but it shall accomplish what I please, and it shall prosper in the thing for
> which I sent it." (Isaiah 55:11)

His Word is perfect for every hungry, listening heart. That is why people will often stop a preacher afterwards and say, "That word was perfect for me," or a new believer may say, "How did that speaker know all that stuff; it was like he was talking straight at me." The person on the platform may not have known anything about them, but trust me, God in Heaven knew and planned the whole thing.

Healthy Houses feed the hungry, because they make a choice to 'prepare for the hungry.' The 'hungry' may be faithful members who have been around for years or they may be brand new people coming through our doors for the first time. The truth is that regardless of how long we have known God, we should never cease to be hungry. Since I began my walk with God at the age of 15, I've hardly missed a Sunday in church. I sit through many multiple services and listen to the same message again and again, but I never cease to glean and receive. Even if I have heard a message a hundred times, I'm hungry for God and therefore find myself fed by my King again and again. I thank Him that I sit in a healthy House that never fails to feed my soul and spirit.

What is laid out on the table has the capacity to strengthen the weak, heal the sick, bandage the broken and gather home the lost. Ezekiel 34 is not for the fainthearted. It contains a sobering reminder of God's attitude towards lazy or neglectful shepherds who do not diligently feed or provide for His children. It says:

> "Son of man, prophesy against the shepherds of Israel, prophesy and say to them, Thus says the Lord God to the shepherds, *"Woe to the shepherds of Israel who **feed themselves!*** Should not the shepherds feed the flocks? You eat the fat and clothe yourselves with wool; you slaughter the fatlings, but you don't feed the flock. The weak you have not strengthened, nor have you healed those who were sick, nor bound up the broken, nor brought back what was driven away, nor sought what was lost; but with force and cruelty you have ruled them." (Ezekiel 34:2)

If you are brave or serious enough, then read the entire chapter and catch a glimpse of God's heart. To Him there is nothing more precious on the earth than His children, regardless of whether or not they are redeemed. I say this often: there are only two categories of people on the earth – *redeemed sons and daughters,* and *unredeemed sons and daughters.* Heaven will boast sons and daughters and sadly, Hell will boast sons and daughters. Our sole responsibility is to turn the scale in favour of Heaven by feeding and loving God's children into such a place of relationship that when they encounter Him face-to-face, He is no stranger.

ONE PURPOSE

The House of God exists for this purpose and this purpose alone – that we might present God's children as a Bride perfected for their Groom. If you have found yourself in ministry, then understand that the ministry is not actually about you. *The Church is not there to serve you, your ego or your lifestyle.* We are there to serve the Church and God's people – to strengthen the weak, heal the sick, bind up the broken, bring back what has been driven away and seek that which is lost. Of course, we find ourselves blessed in the process, because there are Heaven-sent benefits that come with being co-labourers with God, but **never forget** what it is truly about, or you just might find yourself labelled with the "Woe to you, shepherds of Israel" category.

Among the words used to define hunger we find *pain, discomfort and exhaustion.* The dictionary also describes hunger as a craving or strong desire. We live in a strange world. It is regarded as common knowledge that there is actually enough food held in storage to feed the world several times over, yet there are many nations on our earth where children die daily for lack of sustenance. We also live in a world where people literally live off the 'fat of the land,' yet their soul and spirit are tragically malnourished. Emotionally and mentally they suffer pain, discomfort and exhaustion.

Jesus came to remedy the problem. After thirty-three years and 'mission accomplished' He departed the planet, however did They (the Father, Son and Holy Spirit) leave us alone? No! They manoeuvred time and history and left us with the ageless and eternal Word of God. The Word Who became flesh and for a season moved into our neighbourhood left, but the Word remains today. It continues to be the planet's bestseller and has the staggering capacity to put 'flesh' on our spiritual person. Healthy Houses understand and are committed to feeding God's children with only the very best available.

A handful of years ago, I found myself in what you might call a Holy Spirit ministry service. As we worshipped and embraced the luxury of lingering in His presence, I felt as though I was at the door of the Throne Room of God. It wasn't a 'full-on, Panasonic colour type' vision, but it was a very strong impression that changed not only me, but many others who I have shared it with. It was as though I was on the threshold of the Throne Room, my toes on the edge and I was peeking in. I then sensed the Holy Spirit come alongside (as He does) and nudge me. He very gently said, "You can go in, you know. You can go in. Sit at His feet. Sit on His knee if you want ... and He will tell you everything you need to know."

That vision, impression, encounter – call it what you wish – has fed my spirit many times. It has sustained me in my journey and encouraged me many times to draw aside and find the fuel, gold or food needful.

A healthy House is distinguished by a well-worn path that leads to the very Throne of God. It lights and leads the way for those whose hunger causes them to search.

CHAPTER TWENTY

HEALTHY HOUSES
ARE THE HOPE OF THE FUTURE

'MY SON, BE ATTENTIVE TO MY WISDOM [GODLY WISDOM LEARNED BY ACTUAL AND COSTLY EXPERIENCE] ...'

[PROVERBS 5:1]

HEALTHY HOUSES
ARE THE HOPE OF THE FUTURE

HOPE — EXPECTATION AND DESIRE OF TRUST, PROMISE,
CONFIDENCE AND POSSIBILITY

Healthy Houses are without doubt the HOPE OF THE FUTURE. We live in a world full of gorgeous people, yet scratch the surface and you will find beautiful but searching hearts *hungry for hope and a reason for their existence.* For such people who suddenly find themselves in 'our world,' it *should be an encounter with **their future**.* They should not enter a world where people eye them sideways or make judgement about their appearance or lifestyle. They should encounter a people who have respect for another's life, regardless of what it may look like, and who are genuinely excited at the prospect of helping them discover their future.

When God prompted me to host a women's conference and call it COLOUR YOUR WORLD, His directive was, "Bobbie, create a conference in Sydney for women … predominantly for young women, but girded about by older, wise women … and tell them that *there is a God in Heaven who believes in them and a company of people down here on earth also believing in them.*"

GOD BELIEVES IN PEOPLE – He believes in their person, He believes in their potential and He believes in their future. I think if all of us could see others through these eyes, it would change the way we deal with our neighbours, our family, our friends, our colleagues and even the strangers we bump into across everyday life.

For each and every one of us, our Heavenly Father has very precise thoughts about tomorrow. He says:

> "I know the thoughts and plans that I have for you … thoughts and plans for welfare and peace and not for evil, to give you hope in your final outcome." (Jeremiah 29:11)

More than our finite minds can really comprehend, God's desire is to establish this FUTURE AND HOPE in all our lives, and so to enter a place that boasts a powerful connection with the future *should, can* and *will* dramatically change a person's perspective on life if all the dynamics come together. So what are these dynamics and how can we partner with God in *presenting His House as an oasis of hope*? Here are a few thoughts.

EMBRACE THEM

Embrace people where they are at, and accept them for who they are. Don't focus on what is missing or not happening in their lives yet. Overseas peers observing Hillsong Church have commented that, generally speaking, we are very embracing of people.

My husband Brian is committed to sending people OUT of church feeling better than when they came IN. Life 'out there' can often be unkind, so when people come to the House of God it should be a pleasant experience. It should be an encounter with hope, encouragement and life (with plenty of love and support thrown in for good measure). Brian and I would not intentionally allow anyone on to our preaching platform who is there for any other reason than to love, bless and build our people. If you are a pastor or leader, when was the last time you *genuinely* told your people that you love them? We don't find it difficult to frequently tell our people that we love them, **because we actually do!** So if you do love them, why don't you verbalise it more often?

LOVE THEM

I invited an interstate friend to speak to our women and as I drove her from the airport, my secretary phoned. I chatted away and then found myself saying, "Okay, you're awesome. Thanks for doing that. I love you!" As I hung up my friend in the passenger seat commented, "Gee, I can't remember the last time I told my P.A. that I loved her." Now you might think that's definitely a 'girl thing' or a 'Bobbie thing.'

No! It's actually a family thing! What's wrong with telling people that you love them? The fact that we constantly tell our people that we love them is not a formula for church growth, nor is it a cliché. We are, I confess, **madly in love with our church** and it creates an environment that God can work in. Without being sickeningly corny or over-the-top, I want those words ('I love you') to be *the full stop* on every encounter. I want my kids to hear those words when they leave the house; I want my husband to hear those words when we part company; I want my friends to be familiar with that little phrase; and I want our church to carry those words away with them when they leave a service.

When people know they are loved and accepted (warts and all) it is definitely easier to smile at the future. Proverbs 31:25 says of the women in the House, "They smile at the future." This became the heartbeat of our 2001 COLOUR YOUR WORLD conference and more than likely will be the title of my book on the Thirty-One Woman. I believe that if we confidently take hold of our King, if we allow His Word to refine our hearts and if we embrace our God-given destiny, we will find ourselves smiling at the future.

GIVE THEM LIGHT

I think that in the days ahead we will encounter Christians walking around with smiles the size of the Pacific Ocean. *Their countenance will radiate God and they'll stand out in a world that is progressively becoming darker.* Their smile will transcend their circumstances and they'll smile even in the midst of persecution and challenge. Why? Because their smile reveals a depth of relationship with a truly amazing God. Isaiah 60:1 exhorts us to arise!

> "Arise [from the depression and prostration in which circumstances have kept you – rise to a new life]! Shine [be radiant with the glory of the Lord], for your light has come, and the glory of the Lord has risen upon you! For behold, darkness shall cover the earth, and dense darkness [*despondency, depression, despair, sadness*] [all] peoples, but the Lord shall arise upon you [O Jerusalem], and His glory shall be seen on you. (Isaiah 61:1,2 AMP)

As darkness envelops people in these coming days, it will be a truly radiant company of people who will be light in the darkness. So don't forget to check what I call your 'God countenance' next time you come to the House of God (or the supermarket or workplace for that matter). You may not feel like smiling, but why not try? When was our Christian testimony ever based on feelings? The Bible frequently tells us to, "Bring the sacrifice, offering or gift of praise to our King." Smile, lift those shoulders, put on God, make the devil nervous and give hope to unbelievers who are venturing into our world. They desperately need to see us *wearing our God well*, so that they too might be drawn to the truth of this Saviour in whom we boast.

Some people may criticise that last comment and say that to do such is a façade. No it is not a façade. A façade is to live a lie. I'm talking about **taking responsibility for the atmosphere in the House**. As a wife, mother and woman of God, I am responsible for the atmosphere in my home regardless of how I feel. I can make it miserable and horrible, or I can (in Christ) make it delightfully irresistible. By the grace of God, I choose the latter and I choose it also for my church and world.

One of the greatest gifts I can give to my husband, children and the people of our church is to LEAD THEM IN THEIR LOVE OF GOD. I can do that by *presenting as a strong, enthused, courageous, rejoicing, faith-filled woman of God*. Sometimes I'll catch my countenance drooping (which is not a sin) and I'll quickly try to correct it with a smile, because regardless of circumstance or whatever, I have a God who is above everything. How can one not wear that truth without it affecting one's entire person?☺ I have a rather vivacious, bubbly, contagious friend called Holly. Some people think she was just born that way, some people tell her she is just "too happy" but the reality is she wakes up each morning like everyone else on the planet – her only difference is that with each new sunrise she DECIDES to be joyful.

SHOW THEM THE WAY

Nothing screams louder in life than *example*! There is nothing more powerful than to hear or see someone generously say, "Here, let me show you the way" or "Do you realise that there is actually *a better way* to do that?"

In language that everyone can understand, Jesus said of Himself, "I am the Way, the Truth and the Life. No man can come to the Father, except through Me." Hey! What's *not* to understand? He is the Way, He is the Truth and He is the Life. If we truly believe these words, then *everything about our lives should give expression to that WAY, TRUTH and LIFE.*

The House of God is about making and presenting A WAY for the world. How better to do that than to *write that truth across our everyday lives.* Signage and posters are cool, but the world is more likely to be moved by connecting with someone who said, "Well, let me tell you something. I was a total mess, I had no hope, no sense of *whatever*, but hey look at me today. I found Jesus and look what He's done for me." So I challenge you as leaders and believers alike, to live your own life in a 'neon-light' fashion – in a manner that screams the reality of an awesome God who is totally pro-humanity.

Regardless of your status in life, regardless of whether you are married or single, divorced or widowed, career or ministry called, I challenge you to live your life in such a way that it testifies and advertises that **there is definitely a better way of doing this adventure called life.**

Outsiders ought to come in and be stunned by people who haven't just decided to get married, but have decided to *stay married.* They should encounter people from every strata of life who are working out (in Christ) how to be *successful and influential.* They should encounter single people who are not only content in their singleness, but who are having such an *incredibly full and fabulous life* that they've forgotten they're even single. I'm labouring these points because this world is full of too many gorgeous people, young in particular, who think life begins and ends with a weekend of bars, booze, shallow nightclubbing and a cheap roll in the sack. But hey, *there is a better way to have fun* and it's a way that doesn't end up in some cheap devaluation of life, carrying the stench of excessive alcohol, vomit or heartless sex, which produces a Monday morning illusion of, "Yeah I had a great time (I think!)"

Hope of a better way really does exist. Jesus knew all about it. Such is the mind-blowing splendour of this hope that He selflessly left his home in Heaven and planted Himself in the middle of broken-down, stench-ridden humanity in a divinely-inspired strategy to reconnect us with this very future and hope. Because of this, countless thousands upon thousands of beautiful people all across this earth are each day coming to a knowledge of this truth, and are *trading a life of hopelessness* for a life that speaks instead of health, contentment, satisfaction and fulfilment.

Healthy Houses have this magnificent hope painted across every nook, cranny and crevice of the House, and are fully equipped should the world come knocking on their door.

CHAPTER TWENTY-ONE

HEALTHY HOUSES ARE
COMMITTED TO THE GENERATIONS

SAFE-KEEPING IS A
GENERATIONAL THING ...

FRAME THEIR FUTURE BEAUTIFULLY!

HEALTHY HOUSES ARE
COMMITTED TO THE GENERATIONS

COMMITTED – TO MORALLY DEDICATE OR PLEDGE TO SAFE KEEPING

O ur annual women's conference in Sydney (that is affectionately called COLOUR) recently produced a brochure in which I gave an entire colour spread to the following words, **"Living life magnificently – it's a generational thing**." A narrow, unexpansive mindset may criticise, "How excessive – fancy wasting a whole page on one statement; how much did that cost anyway?" I refuse to bow to that narrow mindset because along with our awesome Heavenly Father, we believe in the future and will at times make bold, calculated and budgeted moves to attach value to human life.

A great and respected man of God in South Africa was once heard to say, "The only time God is extravagant is when it comes to sinners – He may send you thousands of miles for ONE sinner." Needless to say that explains His reasoning for sending His priceless, only-begotten Son to rescue generations of humanity.

To live with an attitude that boldly says, "*I will live this gift of life magnificently*" will without doubt affect life and the generations following. When I began writing this chapter, I was in a hotel room far away from home as a guest speaker at a conference. I put the television on to provide a little noise and company. One of those 'reality' TV-shows came on (along the lines of *The Jerry Springer Show*) where men, women and teenagers (who are supposed to be family) will whine, fight, hurl abuse and literally pull each others' hearts to pieces in front of a watching world. I know that everyone isn't necessarily like this, but you have to agree that television culture is changing rapidly. What is classified as 'real life' television has become addictive and people will sit passively in their lounge rooms glued to television sets watching other people attack life in a way that is anything but impressive.

Christians who live sheltered lives need to know that 'the world' is becoming somewhat of a zoo. While there is still much good out there, *behaviour patterns* for the majority are rapidly deteriorating because many of the absolutes of life are effectively being eroded. The devil is no fool. He knows that his time is short and he is working overtime to make his effect known. I find this almost incomprehensible, but churches still exist who are more concerned with contending over the colour of the carpet, or whether or not the pews should stay, or whether or not drums and guitars are from the devil, or whether or not women can be involved in Kingdom matters – while a stone's throw away, people are literally destroying themselves and their children because they don't know that there is a better way. And the longer these precious people don't hear, *the more ingrained the problems become.*

OUR CHALLENGE

This chapter is simply to challenge your mindset to the reality that as God's representatives on planet earth, **we have a very large responsibility to set the planet in order for the sake of those following.** If we don't pick up that challenge, honestly where will it all end?

So where does restoration begin? How can you and I (and our seemingly little world of influence) set the planet right? Well – it begins with us.

My husband has always said that revival begins in our heart. Our responsibility is to *get it right*, so that those following can *get it right*. I was teaching our women recently about 'first generation Christians.' First generation Christians are those who are the first off the rank in their family as far as salvation goes. If you want to use your imagination, it's like the Spirit of God said, "Okay – see that one down there, start with him or her." Bingo! You respond and salvation enters your heart. But hey, that is just the beginning. Being born again is always just the beginning. The real adventure begins as you allow the redemptive process to begin.

So assuming that all your ancestors *were not perfect* – here's a thought: As a First Generation Christian, YOU GET TO SET THE FAMILY IN ORDER! Yes,

YOU get to deal with all the generational junk. YOU get to handle all the nonsense, abuse and generational curses that have been handed down in your family. YOU get to re-write the history pages of your family. Let me say that again – YOU get to rewrite the history pages of your family! Up until this point, your family may have had a history of divorce, anger or abusive behaviour, but it changes when you say, "By the Grace of God, I'm rewriting the book. I'm turning the page and my family, my world, my sphere, my generation are going to walk into A WHOLE NEW FUTURE!"

Then you, like the Psalmist, can boast, "This generation will tell of God's great goodness from one generation to the next" (Psalm 145: 4).

I think this is so powerful. My husband has preached for many years on this subject, so for example: Your family may have been plagued by divorce, after divorce, after divorce, but then you changed the pattern. You found the keys and began a new pattern of long-and-happy-marriage, followed by long-and-happy-marriage, followed by long-and-happy marriage. Or in your family it may have been an issue of repetitive alcohol and addiction, but you introduced freedom and liberty to the generations following. (Brian wrote about this in his book called *You can Change the Future* – perhaps this book may help if this scenario relates to you or someone else you love.)

As those who love and adore our King, may we be a people who press in and access His Grace to enable us to live like this. I pray that our churches (our Houses) will produce awesome *men, women and children* of a different calibre, who have the capacity to frame their future beautifully. Without being too lengthy, here is what we can do.

MAY OUR MEN RISE UP AND BE MEN!

This subject is truly a book in itself! Before I go any further, I have to say that in the environment from which I come, we love our men. They are all men in the truest sense of the word. Of course they're not perfect (☺) but they are committed to this journey of life. Have they made mistakes? I dare say they have. Are they willing to grow and mature? Absolutely! So when I venture to say, "May our men rise up and be men," it is simply a prayer that they would truly *rise to the stature of their created potential.*

As I have already mentioned, I teach the women of our church on a regular basis. Recently we have spent a considerable amount of time studying the 'Proverbs Thirty-One woman.' If you dare read this strategically-placed final chapter in the

MALE BY BIRTH, MEN BY CHOICE

[DR EDWIN LOUIS COLE]

book described as the Book of Wisdom (written by a man who has been declared as the wisest, wealthiest and most creative man of all time) you find an incredible challenge or charge to humankind – men, women and youth alike. It boldly challenges *young and older men* to realise that life is not about fast living and fast women, but rather that they were **created to be princes and kings on the earth** – princes who realise what life is really about, princes who realise that they are the sons of a King, princes who realise that life is actually about *opening your mouth with truth and executing justice on the earth,* princes who know how to *find and partner with great women.* That may sound terribly romantic (especially if you're a woman who is married to a man who cannot move his butt off the couch), but nonetheless IT'S IN THE BIBLE. The reality of it manifests in men (young and old alike) who therefore live their lives brilliantly.

They don't *squander their potential* on wasteful living. They don't make *stupid decisions* because they're thinking with out-of-control, below-the-waist hormones, and they don't *jeopardise their 'magnificent ending'* because of lack of wisdom. Such men are delightfully irresistible to both women and the Father Himself. These men are not afraid to discover WHO THEY ARE IN CHRIST and because of this, we encounter men who are walking the planet with a sense of origin and purpose that confounds 21st Century human logic, negates stupid decisions and results in magnificence at every level – marriage, relationships, youthful energy, fatherhood, career, ministry and eternal impact.

Such men will rewrite the history pages with excellence, and I know that Heaven will smile with admiration and praise.

MAY OUR WOMEN WALK IN THEIR CREATED PURPOSE

This is another huge subject and one worthy of what will probably constitute my next book on the 'Thirty-One Woman.' I am discovering that the thought of *women being permitted to walk in their created purpose* is rather fresh on the planet. That is not to say that God has not had **His girls** strategically placed in time and history, or that He has not tried to establish this truth across the centuries, but as a way of life and thinking, and as a mindset within the Church, this sadly is not the experience of many women.

I live in Australia, which, generally speaking, is a peaceful and beautiful environment. People are not oppressed, life basically has no ceilings and if you desire to achieve as a woman, then the sky is your limit. However this is not the case for every female on the earth. In certain parts of the earth, if you are a woman, your value is not much higher than that of an animal. They live a life of humiliation and oppression, and countless thousands are mutilated every day for their femininity.

In many places the issue of 'women in leadership' and 'women in the Kingdom' is still a hot issue among some. There are many pockets of traditional or religious Christianity which also regard women with disdain. The very suggestion of them being created to be **Kingdom partners** is met with abhorrence.

Jesus Christ was the greatest emancipator of women – He believed in them, He released them, He facilitated their gift and talent, He depended on them. He allowed them to support His ministry, His heart melted when they loved and adored Him, and to put it all in perspective, He died for them as much as He died for our male counterparts. Hideous, dark mindsets that *crush womanhood under oppression* (be that at the hand of cruel dictators and culture or at the hand of mindless, heartless men within the privacy of homes) are nothing more than demonic- inspired forces purposed to undermine the potential of **God's beautiful girls**. May we never forget that these beautiful girls just happen to represent and constitute over one half of the planet's population, and within the Church, one half of the *Bride of Christ.*

If you have never seen it this way, then I challenge you for the sake of the truth and the gospel to get with the plan and enter the light of the 21st Century. When God created Eve, she was *a gift* given to Adam – a beautifully refined gift created in the image of God Himself. She was fashioned not from dust but from Adam's own flesh. *Men or nations that disregard the value of this precious gift (regardless of their redemptive status) are asking for trouble.*

1 Peter 3:7 says that men and women are created as *"joint heirs* of the grace." Meditate on that for a moment and think about its consequence. This issue of *placing value upon womanhood* burns in my spirit and is a strong and heightened message emerging across the earth. My husband, who is totally amazing at releasing women, recently made a powerful comment. He said that over the past five years the Hillsong Church has basically doubled. He attributed this growth to the fact that in this time, I have been actively investing into women at both a local level in our House, and also nationally and internationally through the COLOUR women's conference. An untuned ear listening may not have caught the depth of what he said, but I did. He wasn't attributing this entire growth to my investment alone, because there are many contributing factors, but rather that because THE HOUSE was **recognising** and **honouring** and **placing value upon womanhood**, it was drawing forth God's attention, blessing and favour. God is a good Father and, like any good father, He places incredible value upon His girls – that is worth meditating upon.

GOD LOVES HIS GIRLS

Our Father in Heaven is desperate to see *strong men and strong women* emerge in the House and across the Kingdom. In Genesis chapter one, we read the story of Creation where God said, "Let us make man in Our image and so He created them *male and female and said to them together - go multiply, be fruitful and have dominion."* In other words He intended us to **rule and reign together.**

I pray that all women will rise to the stature of being mature women in the House. I also have no problem exhorting women to become Kingdom partners, because our experience has revealed that this revelation produces wonderful fruit.

At the time of writing this chapter, I can testify that in every key area of church life at Hillsong Church, we have women in *key positions of responsibility.* Are these positions of authority? Yes, because responsibility requires authority. As women we have no problem with submission and we are all submitted to the mission of the House. Submission simply means to come 'under the mission' of something. I know these women have no problem coming under the mission of Hillsong Church because our mission and mandate is exciting, liberating and awesome. And because of this I believe that our House is flourishing with health.

As women, we complete the picture and this is the prevailing spirit writing itself across the women of our church. None of us are trying to lord it over anyone, because we are basically *'whatever-it-takes women'.* We will do whatever it takes and we will do it with willing hearts. If we find ourselves preaching and teaching, we will do it with all our heart. If we find ourselves serving or supporting we will do that also with all of our heart. It is honestly not a big deal.

Our spiritual DNA defines us as **helper**. Helper literally means 'one who comes alongside, who helps, who is prepared to stand in the gap if need be, and one who is prepared to be a blessing.' It's really not difficult, and if men and women across the Church of Jesus Christ *could keep the equation this simple,* then health and wholeness, life and liberty, would find its way into their experience.

As women, we are created to be nothing less than a blessing. (Remember that the word blessing in the Amplified Bible includes being happy, fortunate and to be envied.)

Is your church producing a generation of women who are happy and enviable, who have others looking on and saying, "Gosh I'll definitely have what she's having! I want her sense of purpose, conviction, resolve and partnership." If all of this is a mystery to you, then perhaps my first book *I'll Have What She's Having* will stretch your thinking to new parameters.

MAY OUR CHILDREN RISE TO THEIR STATURE

I love the thought of magnificent, functional children. We've already chatted in the first part of this book about healthy families, yet something phenomenal is happening across the earth – **a youth generation are emerging which is different from any generation before.** They are the fruit of a fast-moving, fast-advancing, highly technical and creative world. In western society in particular, they are educated and resourced like none before them. Because of this, I believe that their gift, their measure and their talent has the capacity to take the Kingdom to places that previous generations have only dreamed about.

I heard someone say that when God is about to do something phenomenal on the earth, He will 'wire' a generation accordingly. I've never forgotten those words and I'm often reminded of them when I observe our youth in action. They fear nothing, they are confident beyond their years, they exude talent and creativity, and they are spontaneous and adventurous. When they get switched on to something, it becomes an all-consuming passion – be that a passion for a rock group, a youth culture *or a Kingdom Cause.*

I believe that in the days ahead, the youth in God's Kingdom will storm the gates of Hell in their own distinctive, aggressive way. It won't be according to what a previous generation has known. It will be *a generation serving their own generation* and it will be amazing. Not one of us can harness the aging process, but we can definitely harness 'old mindsets' which limit the potential of the youth in the Kingdom. The goal is always that each generation will acquire more and more wisdom, and then will hand the baton of wisdom on to the next generation. Handing the baton on has nothing to do with methods or structure. It has to do with handing on the 'tools of life' so effectively that the generation following has the wisdom to negotiate the territory that is theirs to walk. We are all writing history's pages and it is up to us to not sabotage our children's opportunity by not preparing them perfectly for what is ahead.

The important things for this youth generation are not the style of their clothes or hair, or whether they have body piercing or not – the issues are 'issues of the heart' and whether or not they have encountered JESUS CHRIST AS LORD. If so, then His Lordship will negotiate their walk. My sons have just entered manhood – they have their own particular style, they are very much the product of their own generation, they still have plenty of growing to do, but their dedication and devotion to their King is breathtaking.

As a natural mother and as a spiritual mum in the House, I live for no other reason than to *equip them perfectly for life*. It begins in the nursery and it continues for the length of their days. A healthy House will facilitate this dream across the breadth of the Church. Gone are the days of 'baby-sitting' the children while their parents are in church. No, we are shaping young men and women of God (young princes and princesses) and must approach children's ministry from this perspective. Our youth are like tender young plants in our hands – our responsibility before God is to shape and fashion them beautifully. Psalm 144 describes the prize: "When our sons are as full grown trees in their youth and our daughters are as pillars as fashioned for a palace" then happy, blessed and prosperous are such a people. It speaks of sons who reach their potential even before adulthood and daughters who are fashioned as for a King. Frame their world like this and they will bring their finest to the planet – *and yet again, another generation will taste Heaven on earth!*

As a leader, facilitate your church accordingly. DO NOT NEGLECT THE YOUNG PEOPLE. Do not neglect them and *then expect them to be in church once adulthood and choice is theirs to decide*. Don't be tempted to keep the children and youth at a distance. I realise church methods and cultures are different across the earth, but a substantial gap is evident whenever I have visited a church that keeps their youth in separate services. I'm not talking about specific youth or children's ministries (which we all facilitate) but rather an inherent health that is felt when young people and adults mix openly and honestly in the House of God.

A healthy House out of its good health will naturally and substantially set up the future beautifully for the generations following. The word 'commit' means 'to morally dedicate or pledge to safekeeping.' As mature adults, this is our God-given mandate from Heaven above.

CHAPTER TWENTY-TWO

HEALTHY HOUSES FUND THE SALVATION OF THE EARTH

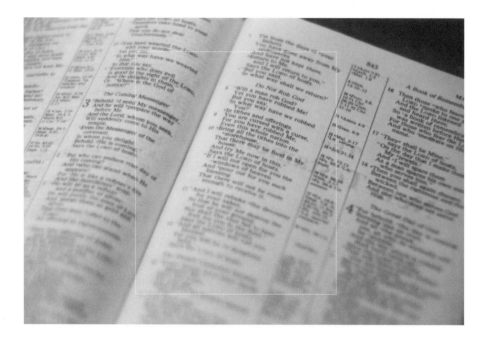

'BRING ALL THE TITHES (THE WHOLE TENTH OF YOUR INCOME)
INTO THE STOREHOUSE, THAT THERE MAY BE FOOD IN MY HOUSE'

[MALACHI 3:10 (AMP)]

HEALTHY HOUSES FUND THE SALVATION OF THE EARTH

FUND — A PERMANENT STOCK OF SOMETHING READY
TO BE DRAWN UPON

W e have so much fun at church. We even have fun when it comes to the offering. Every week in one of our many weekend services, you can almost guarantee that my darling husband will get up and say – "Okay, turn to Malachiiiiiiiiii …" And everyone will shout back: "THREEEEE!!!!"

I'm sure Malachi Chapter Three is one passage of scripture that gives the devil a great headache. If you are unfamiliar or uncomfortable at the thought of bringing up the subject of finance, please, PLEASE don't switch off here. This chapter is so important because it has to do with funding the salvation of the earth. It is about being sure that when we get to Heaven we don't find 'empty seats' with a sign that says, "They're not here because the finance wasn't released to find them." Now, don't tell me that perhaps that isn't a possibility. Surely God is a God of love and everybody has an opportunity to hear the truth? I hope I'm mistaken, but even as I write this chapter, statistics tell me that there are millions of people in the 'unreached category.' That's the category of people who have never *even **heard** the name of Jesus*, so even as you read this, some of them will pass on into eternity. There are some things our minds will not understand until we see our Creator face to face.

God is a just and righteous judge, but Jesus came for a lost and dying world that was hell-bound and He said, "Pray, pray, **pray** to the Lord of the Harvest, that He would thrust more labourers into the field" (Matthew 9:38).

Labourers are not merely those who say yes to the calling of the mission field, but labourers are men and women who are prepared to say YES to whatever God requires of them. For some, this will literally be a mission field in a foreign nation. For others, it will be involvement in ministry at local church level, and for yet others, it will mean *rising to the stature of your financial potential* so that you can contribute *big bucks* to the extension of God's Kingdom.

I'm sure that your true heart is to see the masses won to Jesus. I don't question this and I am certainly not trying to preach to you. All I want to do is draw attention to what is important. If anything, I'm stirring my own heart here and my deep desire is that every single person in my own church will find the wherewithal to pick up this book and be encouraged to press on deeper in God.

In Malachi 3, we find a compilation of words that have the capacity to rock the world. This is what God says: "Bring all the tithes and all the offerings *into the storehouse*, that there *might be food in my House* and prove Me in this, that I will not open for you the windows of Heaven and pour out such blessing that you will not be able to contain it." Not only that, but our amazing God promises also to rebuke the devourer on our behalf.

"Bring all the tithes and all the offerings into the storehouse." The whole purpose of the tithe and the offering is that the House (the storehouse) might be full so that it might be *fully equipped and fully resourced with everything needful to reach humanity.* As the definition at the beginning of this chapter suggests, that it might be "a store waiting to be drawn upon."

KNOCK, KNOCK

For a moment indulge my imagination. Imagine 'the outside world' rolling up to our door and knocking. We answer the door and there stands a beautiful but perhaps tentative person in need. With a smile we ask, "How can we help you?" When someone needs our help, how awesome to be able to help them because we are fully prepared. Perhaps they need help in their marriage? Our response can be, "Hey, we have plenty of people ready to help you be amazing in that area." They may need someone to show them how to be a great parent? Our response, "No problem, we have wonderful programs designed exactly for that purpose." Perhaps they need financial help because they can't pay their electricity bill or have no food? Our response, "Well, because the 'store' is ready and the 'spiritual fridge' is permanently full, we are not only equipped to help, but we also consider it an honour to help."

I honestly believe this is how the Father would have us *manage His House.* You may have heard it said before: The Gospel is free, but it costs a fortune to get it out. That is actually very true. While it costs you and me nothing but time, energy and a little inclination to share our story with a person we might meet, *to spread the gospel powerfully and effectively across the earth costs dollars* – BIG DOLLARS.

REVIVAL COSTS MONEY

To 'house revival' also costs money. When the revival waves seriously begin to roll in, it will cost a phenomenal amount of dollars to build facilities to house the masses. The attitude of some Christians towards Kingdom prosperity never ceases to amaze us. They cry out for revival, but haven't worked out how to tithe and give yet. If the revival they give lip service to actually turned up on their doorstep, they'd get the shock of their lives. They wouldn't have a clue *what to do with all the people,* let alone *where to put them* because they have not personally harnessed any truth about Kingdom finance, and therefore they have no means to resource what is required.

My husband wrote a great book called *You Need More Money* and the entire tenor of it is to see finance released for the extension of the Kingdom. In some quarters, it has made some people very angry. They read it as 'self needs more money,' instead of seeing it as an opportunity to bless others. The reality is that **we all need more money to accomplish God's purposes on the earth.** As I have heard Brian and many others often say, "Money says to a missionary, I can send you. Money says to a needy person, I can help you. Money says to a building, I can build you. Money says to a vision, I can fulfil you." Godly Kingdom prosperity is not about 'self' – it is about winning and making disciples of the lost.

POSITION YOURSELF UNDER AN OPEN HEAVEN

A Healthy House will realise this mandate. She won't *argue or resist or fight.* She'll align herself with the timeless Word of God, she'll rise to the challenge, and she'll teach, encourage and exhort her people to be Kingdom-minded people who put God first in everything, including their finances.

The Word does not lie and *it does deliver.* Churches that get a revelation of Kingdom finance find themselves blessed. They get counted among those who are making a difference in the world. They experience the devourer being rebuked over their lives. They find themselves living under an open Heaven of blessing and they cause the Father to smile in delight that He has found a company of believers who are *prepared to give their all*. He looks down from Heaven and He is very mindful of their coming and going. He watches over their families and their homes. He is acquainted with their workplace and their desires; He is prepared to bless them beyond their wildest dreams because they have chosen to be a people who forever and always put His Kingdom first.

When we get to Heaven, I wonder if the angels of God will not spend a good part of eternity introducing us to strangers who found their way Home because *someone cared enough to sow spiritual seed, in the form of finance, into their salvation.*

There is a great saying I love when it comes to the giving of offerings and finance, "It may leave your hand, but it will never leave your life." When we honour God and release our money, it falls from our hand and becomes spiritual seed on the earth, but as far as Heaven's chronicles go, it is credited to our heavenly account.

When it comes to my life, I strongly desire to be among those whom God can count on. I pray that in your sphere of influence you also will be a magnificent channel of blessing. I challenge you to write yourself into history by being among those who helped fund the Salvation of the earth . There will be people who will be eternally grateful for your investment. Remember the words that were the prompting for this book: "When I call them a House, it is about seriously impacting the world!"

And may I gently remind you that the scripture says that the "Kingdom of Heaven suffers violence and the violent take it by force" (Matthew 11:12). If we are going to produce a company of believers who are Kingdom-minded and who are *full of His Kingdom*, then it stands to reason that from time to time they might encounter violent opposition especially when their endeavours begin to advance into enemy territory. Let's never forget that our job is to take back what the enemy has stolen. Therefore we are to neither faint nor fear, but we are to simply become *stronger than the attack*. Perfect!

THE POTENTIAL
OF A HEALTHY HOUSE

My prayer as we turn the page and begin to bring this book to a conclusion is that *history's pages and Heaven's chronicles will say of the Hillsong Church (and your church)* that …

- THEY BECAME A TRUE FRIEND OF GOD!

- THEY CHANGED HUMANITY'S COURSE!

- THEY SHUT THE MOUTHS OF LIONS!

- THEY DIVERTED EVIL ON THE EARTH!

- THEY RAN A RESCUE SHOP AN INCH FROM HELL!

- THEY MADE GOD FAMOUS THROUGHOUT ALL THE EARTH!

- THEIR EXPLOITS CAUSED HEAVEN TO CHEER!

- AND THEY SERVED THEIR MOMENT WELL!

A KING'S HOUSE

A KING'S HOUSE

KING — A SOVEREIGN, ROYAL POWER WITH SUPREMACY
IN RESPECT OF EXCELLENCE, POWER AND AUTHORITY!

I can hardly believe I am on my last chapter. I began writing this several hundred thousand feet above sea level, en route to Scotland. It has been a wonderful journey (the book – not the flight) and I hope that your heart has been enlarged. I feel that I have fallen in love with you and your world – which is really bizarre considering I possibly don't even know who you are. Nevertheless you are still holding this book and we have come this far together.

A Healthy House is a King's House! How does a mere mortal such as myself give expression to such a statement? How do I, without the help of the Holy Spirit, give expression to this thing that burns in my heart? How will my written words give honour to my King?

A few years ago, a great friend in ministry visited our church and made a statement that has stayed in my heart ever since. He is a wonderful teacher and communicator and has a respected prophetic/visionary gift on his life. On this particular occasion, he stood on the platform, eyeballed our people and said, "God is going to make this church a King's House. A King's House! A House fit for a King, and it will become a benchmark for others. Others will see what a King's House should look like and will model themselves on it." I'll never forget those words. I'm sure those words have been spoken over many others at various times and in various places, but they pierced my heart because in all honesty, it was around the same time that God was prompting me with the subject matter of this book.

A King's House – a house fit for a King. Where shall we begin? Could it be a House that truly reflects His nature, character and love? Could it be a House that truly makes famous His name, His splendour and His majesty? Could it be a House whose heart beats in perfect time with His? A House that is beautiful beyond measure and which reflects with perfection His creativity? A House that lives and moves and has its being in Him? A House empowered with authority, which in turn has the capacity to execute justice and truth on the earth? A House marked with Heaven-inspired compassion which can effectively draw mankind within her walls and then lavish them with love and embrace? A House that can both humbly and proudly boast that **Heaven is in her midst**.

I live for that day. I live for the day that my church, my world, my sphere, and my little piece of accountability before God can boast this in its entirety. I live for the day when *the men and women, children and youth* of our church become a living, breathing expression of their King, without compromise or hindrance, bringing Salvation and Light to every person who comes near their shadow.

I pray that you and your world will rise to this same challenge, and that together we might PREPARE A WAY for our magnificent King to come. "The Spirit and the Bride *(that's you and me)* say, "Come. Come everyone who is thirsty and let them drink of the water of life freely" (Revelation 22:17).

Thank you Father for the gift of your Son. Thank you Jesus for coming. Thank you Holy Spirit that you will carry us to that perfect day. We long for Your Presence and we long to see You face to face alongside the countless multitudes who are our brothers and sisters.

So be blessed my friend. I have loved talking with you, I pray God's perfect Will into your world and I'll catch up with you in Heaven, if not before ☺!

Love,

Bobbie

POSTSCRIPT

A MALE PERSPECTIVE

MY GORGEOUS MAN!

A MALE PERSPECTIVE

———

I thought I'd add a *male perspective* from my awesome husband. Brian and I are Kingdom partners who are loving and pursuing the same thing. What follows are his thoughts on what it takes to make such a magnificent vision reality.

Some years ago, a powerful description of the Church flowed from my husband's lips. The Word exhorts us, "Write the vision, make it plain" (Habbakuk 2:2). Our church has a *strategic mission statement* which is, "To reach and influence the world by building a large Bible-based church, changing mindsets and empowering people to lead and impact in every sphere of life," yet **The Church That I See** has become the *heartfelt vision statement* that motivates our church to continually push out the boundaries.

In early 2001, Brian framed it yet again to an auditorium packed with the leaders of Hillsong Church.

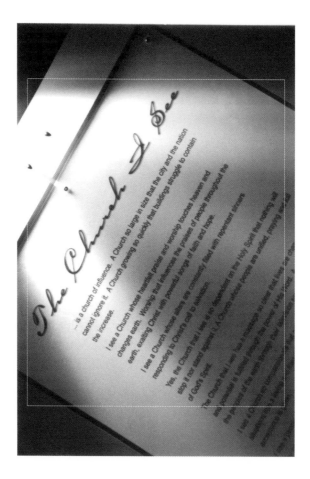

"THE CHURCH THAT I SEE"

BY BRIAN HOUSTON

———

'The Church that I see is a Church of influence. A Church so large in size that the city and nation cannot ignore it. A Church growing so quickly that buildings struggle to contain the increase.

I see a Church whose heartfelt praise and worship touches Heaven and changes earth. Worship which influences the praises of people throughout the earth, exalting Christ with powerful songs of faith and hope.

I see a Church whose altars are constantly filled with repentant sinners responding to Christ's call to salvation.

Yes, the Church that I see is so dependent on the Holy Spirit that nothing will stop it nor stand against it.

A Church whose people are unified, praying and full of God's Spirit.

The Church that I see has a message so clear that lives are changed forever and potential is fulfilled through the power of His Word. A message beamed to the peoples of the earth through their television screens.

I see a Church so compassionate that people are drawn from impossible situations into a loving and friendly circle of hope, where answers are found and acceptance is given.

I see a people so Kingdom-minded that they will count whatever the cost and pay whatever the price to see revival sweep this land.

The Church that I see is a Church so committed to raising, training and empowering a leadership generation to reap the end-time harvest that all its ministries are consumed with this goal.

The Church that I see is a Church whose head is Jesus, whose help is the Holy Spirit and whose focus is the Great Commission.

Yes, the Church that I see could well be our church – Hillsong Church.'

———

‘**P**salm 92:13 says, "Those who are planted in the house of the Lord shall flourish."As leaders in His House, we always need to remember the bottom line of why we are here and what we are doing it for. Written and hung on the walls of both our worship centres is a reminder of the vision, which concludes with – "I see a Church whose head is Jesus, whose help is the Holy Spirit and whose focus is the Great Commission." If we can ensure that this is *always* where we are pointed, then our church will stay on track. The following is based on a simple acronym of the name of our church – HILLSONG.

H IS FOR HEARTFELT

I see a Church whose **heartfelt** praise and worship touches Heaven and changes earth. Worship which influences the praises of people throughout the earth, exalting Christ with powerful songs of faith and hope.

This vision of 'The Church That I See' was written *before* our praise and worship had the kind of influence and impact it is having now. As long as our praise and worship is 'heartfelt' it will always have impact. The key is 'heartfelt.' It is not just about excellence, or how good the musicians are, but it is all about the heart of the worshippers.

No matter what you do or where you sit in our services, you have a role to play because you are also called to be a *leader in worship.* I'm not talking about your musical ability, but taking on the responsibility of leading others into worship by your example. Here are some truths about heartfelt praise and worship:

- *Heartfelt worship reflects the spirit and life of the church.* People sometimes wonder if Hillsong would still be a great church without the worship team. I believe it would, because great worship doesn't exist on its own. There is always a great church behind great worship.

- *Heartfelt worship reflects spontaneity –* an atmosphere where anything can happen and it probably will!

- *Heartfelt worship should fill the hearts and mouths of the people.* Not just the singing of words or the going through of motions, but rather it is reflective of the core of the people.

- *Heartfelt worship is contagious.* It grabs the attention of others and draws them to God.

- And most important – *heartfelt worship always exalts Jesus!*

I IS FOR IMPREGNABLE

*Yes, the Church that I see is so **dependent** on the Holy Spirit that nothing will stop it nor stand against it. A Church whose people are **unified**, **praying** and full of God's Spirit.*

Impregnable means strong and fortified, reflecting a church where nothing can stop it, or stand against it and "where no weapon formed against it will prosper" (Isaiah 54:17). I believe there are three aspects to being impregnable:

- **Dependent** – While so many people try to be so independent, let us never forget that our strength and dependency is totally on the Holy Spirit.

- **Unified** – We must always fight for unity because there is nothing more tragic than a church that is in division and strife. We need to appreciate our unity because it takes a lot of people dying to a lot of things to build a unified church. The Word says that unity is where the Lord commands His blessing. We have a strong church comprised of a strong eldership and a staff that is strong. The enemy would love to attack our church by bringing division, but unity keeps it impregnable.

- **Prayer** – We each need to take on the responsibility of praying for our church. As our whole church only comes together a couple of times a year, we all need to be people of prayer. It is a presumptuous church that never prays. Always be faithful and diligent to pray for the health and soul of our church.

L IS FOR LOVING

*I see a Church so compassionate that people are drawn from impossible situations into a **loving** and friendly circle of hope, where answers are found and acceptance is given.*

A church where answers are found and acceptance is given – these are crucial keys for a great church. Instead of the type of care that only relieves problems, we need to have the kind of care that gives answers. We are committed to building programs across our city that will care for the needs of the community. We are committed to developing new models of care for our community that will provide long-term answers and take people where they should be.

It is a total fallacy when people think that a big church cannot be friendly. Anyone can find someone to make friends with in a large crowd. It's all about sowing in and being friendly. We are not about being a big structure, but the bigger we get, the more important it is that we get smaller at the same time. This is why our cell groups are such an important part of our church.

L IS FOR LEADERSHIP

*The Church that I see is a Church so committed to raising, training and empowering a **leadership** generation to reap the end-time harvest, that all its ministries are consumed with this goal.*

Raising, training and empowering leaders represents the bottom line of what we are doing. Youth groups are fantastic nurseries for emerging leaders. So many of our key pastors originally sharpened their leadership potential through their involvement in youth.

Leadership is to be exemplified, and is always about example. We are committed to releasing people into their gifts, and cells are great for that purpose. They are an environment where individuals can make their contribution to their church.

A leader is one whose life is an example to others – that people might see what we have and want it as well. We need to keep that 'envy factor' alive. It's not about possessions or how much money we have, but it's about people being inspired because we are reaching great levels that they can aspire to also. Leadership is always about giving people something to follow.

S IS FOR SIGNIFICANT

*The Church that I see is a church of **influence**. A Church so large in size that the city and the nation cannot ignore it. A Church growing so quickly that buildings struggle to contain the increase.*

Our church is certainly growing so much that our buildings are struggling to contain the increase. Having multiple services over the weekends is a current solution, but our buildings are reaching the point of struggling to contain the potential growth.

Significance is far more important than fame or prominence. I looked up in the Thesaurus, and synonyms for 'significant' are weighty, substantial, historical. I believe that as we grow in the future, we can build a church that can make history in this nation. The enemy would hate to see this happen and if you lose focus or become distracted, it won't happen. But we can make history!

In the first three months of 2001, our website had over eight million hits. That represents hundreds of thousands of people across the globe investigating our site and looking at what our church is doing. Yet what we are doing is not about our size or prominence, but it is all about the Kingdom and being significant for the Cause of Christ.

O IS FOR OUTREACH

I see a Church whose altars are constantly filled with **repentant sinners** responding to Christ's call to salvation.

We should never take for granted the salvations or altar calls in our services. We will always be committed to seeing people come to Jesus.

We always need to be 'bringers.' As leaders we can feel that one graduates to a level that exempts one from bringing people, but we always need to see it as the prize.

The challenge is never to get self-centred about our Christianity where it is all about us. Our focus must always be 'outward' and always about reaching others.

We need to take responsibility for creating an environment and atmosphere that people want to come to. It is exciting to see people of influence in politics, sport and entertainment being raised up and drawn to our church.

N IS FOR NORMAL AND NATURAL

The Church that I see has a message so clear that lives are changed forever and potential is fulfilled through the power of His Word. A message beamed to the peoples of the earth through their television screens.

I believe we need to develop *the art of making Christianity normal.* It is an exceptional gift that enables a person to come across as spiritual and normal at the same time. One of the hallmarks of our church is that we have a great spiritual church life, but it is fun too. This church is a very cool place to be!

I believe church should be enjoyed, not endured! If it was just 'natural,' it would be a club, and if it was just about being 'spiritual,' we may as well go straight to Heaven. What we are about is 'bringing His world to our world' and about turning upside-down thinking right side up (worldly thinking to God's way of thinking).

We represent the greatest life of all, and it should be normal and natural. Everything we do should appeal to the Mr & Mrs Average Person and make them want to know God too.

G IS FOR GENEROUS

I see a people so **Kingdom-minded** that they will count whatever the cost and pay whatever the price to see revival sweep this land.

A church of generous people are prepared to count the cost and pay whatever to see God's purposes come to pass. People talk about wanting revival and get a shock when they see what it looks like. In reality, revival brings a level of discomfort and being generous is more about 'attitude' than it is about finances.

As our church continues to grow and expand, we need to maintain a spirit that is constantly looking outward and onward. Instead of small, contained thinking, we need to reflect a spirit that is prepared to constantly lay down one's life for the Kingdom.

Yes, the Church that I see could well be our church – Hillsong Church.'

[BRIAN HOUSTON, APRIL 2001]

CD COMPILATION

I simply thought it would be great to put the sound of the House upon this book. Of course my challenge was, "Which songs shall I choose?" This compilation simply felt right at the time. Play it in your home or car, and may your spirit rise in adoration and prayer.

1. "On the Lords Day" – because it steals my heart. I play it continually in my car and it causes everything within to pray that His Kingdom will come. Had to start there!
©1999 Reuben Morgan/Hillsong Publishing. As recorded on *United Live – Everyday*, courtesy of Hillsong Music Australia

2. "Heaven" – because it is just so beautiful. How can you write a book about Heaven on earth and not include this one?
©1998 Reuben Morgan/Hillsong Publishing. As recorded on *United Live – Everyday*, courtesy of Hillsong Music Australia

3. "God is Moving" – because I love our youth and I love their raw passion for God. It may be a little 'youthie' for some, but listen for the sound of revival. It's more than lyrics and noise – it's a youth generation hungry for the footsteps of God.
©1999 Marty Sampson/Hillsong Publishing. As recorded on *United Live – Everyday*, courtesy of Hillsong Music Australia

4. "Dwelling Places" – because the first time we sang this song, I honestly felt that we were in the company of angels.
©1999 Miriam Webster/Hillsong Publishing. As recorded on *By Your Side*, courtesy of Hillsong Music Australia

5. "Reaching for You" – because it makes you want to fling wide your arms and dance with God.
©2000 Ray Badham/Hillsong Publishing. As recorded on *For This Cause*, courtesy of Hillsong Music Australia

6. "Dwell in Your House" – because that is the constant desire of my heart.
©2000 Paul Ewing/Hillsong Publishing. As recorded on *For This Cause*, courtesy of Hillsong Music Australia

7. "One Day" – because one day in the House of God is totally better than a thousand anywhere else!
©2000 Reuben Morgan/Hillsong Publishing. As recorded on *For This Cause*, courtesy of Hillsong Music Australia

8. "Jesus Generation" – because who can resist the thought of a risen King and His Glory! As far as I'm concerned "Emmanuel always and forever!"
©2000 Reuben Morgan/Hillsong Publishing. As recorded on *United Live – Best Friend*, courtesy of Hillsong Music Australia

For further information
on other books and resource material by
Brian & Bobbie Houston,
contact:
Maximised Leadership Inc.
PO Box 1195, Castle Hill NSW 1765 Australia
www.maximisedleadership.com